FOSTERING
LEADERSHIP
SKILLS
IN MINISTRY

JEAN MARIE HIESBERGER

D1026391

Liguori
LIGUORI, MISSOURI

Imprimi Potest:
Richard Thibodeau, C.Ss.R.
Provincial, Denver Province
The Redemptorists

Published by Liguori Publications
Liguori, Missouri
www.liguori.org
www.catholicbooksonline.com

Library of Congress Control Number: 2002115570
ISBN 0-7648-0847-8

Printed in the United States of America
07 06 05 04 03 5 4 3 2 1
First edition

Dedication

~

I dedicate this book to the two loves with whom my life has been blessed.

To my husband, Bob Heyer, who for more than thirty years has been a partner in life and a partner in ministry. The challenges on the path of our life together have been not only more manageable but occasions of real learning, and its joys much deeper because of him.

To my daughter, Kristin Heyer who, from the day of her birth, has truly amazed me, delighted me, and taught me so much. I look forward to a future rich with even more of these same gifts.

Contents

∼

Introduction

~

"Go forth and bear fruit!" the gospel charges us. Each person lives out this mandate in a unique way. For to live it fully is to honor our own unique mission. And our personal mission integrates our values, our talents, and our skills. Furthermore, our mission is different for each person just as it different for each community. This is so because we have been placed in a particular spot on our planet and at a certain unique moment in history and charged to discover and live out the story of our life there.

Yet each of us has the same mission, for we share the mission of Christ. As an individual, as a community, as a church we all share the mission of announcing the Good News, bringing about the kingdom as best we can. We do this in our personal life. We do this in our life together as a community.

While we may never do it perfectly, we can do it well. And the reason we are confident of that is that we do not walk alone. We walk with the life of the Spirit in us and with our community around us. We carry along with us the treasure of talents that God has put at our disposal. In parish ministry it is up to us to honor those talents and to develop the skills needed for pastoral planning, working with volunteers, developing small community groups, leading meetings or any of the myriad steps we take to further Christ's mission.

This little volume is a gathering of some of the things I have learned through my teaching, research, and most especially what parishioners and parish leaders have taught me. It is what so many committed people are doing to develop their skills and their relationships with each other in order to more effectively "Go forth and bear fruit!"

JEAN MARIE HIESBERGER

CHAPTER 1

Jesus As Servant-Leader: Becoming One of Them to Lead Them

～

For I have set you an example, that you also should do as I have done to you. Very truly, I tell you, servants are not greater than their master, nor are messengers greater than the one who sent them. If you know these things, you are blessed if you do them.

JOHN 13:15–17

Christians naturally look to Jesus as the model for living a good and moral life. They study the example of how he lived to find direction for themselves, and they reflect on his words and teachings to discover what he taught about the expectations of those who call themselves "Christian." What did Christ's actions and words teach Christians about how they are supposed to live? The lifelong process of studying Jesus is especially important for those who are leaders in the Christian community.

But who are such leaders in the Church today? When I presented this question to a Roman Catholic bishop, he responded that a leader is simply anyone who has followers. Some people seem to naturally attract people to follow them for a variety of reasons. Other people, we notice, are leaders by virtue of the position they hold or the role they perform in the community. They may be elected or appointed or hired into the position. In the best of cases, our leaders are both: that is, they have the qualities that make others want to follow them, and they are in positions to exercise those qualities and talents for the good of the community.

In our parishes and dioceses we see both kinds of leaders—some of both kinds, leaders by talent and leaders by position. We also experience many styles of leadership. There are positions in the parish, for example, that are obviously leadership positions: pastors, pastoral administrators, parish council members, associate pastors and pastoral ministers, principals, directors of religious education (DREs), volunteer coordinators. These and many other positions can indicate leadership roles. Some leaders in the parish are salaried; some are volunteers; some are full-time employees. Regardless of these differences, having the qualities of a good leader clearly enhances one's effectiveness in any leadership role.

Leaders come in many shapes and sizes, styles, and personalities. Leadership is not, for example, about being an extrovert or an introvert. I met a pastor in Texas who filled the room with his personality and energy wherever he went. When I observed his parishioners' loyalty and commitment, I could only think of the Pied Piper. Most people would have followed him wherever he chose to lead them. This man was an especially good leader because he led people not to himself but beyond that, to a vision and a belief in their own power and understanding of their Christian duty. They were a people who were energized and confident, shaping their parish into a Christian community.

Likewise, I also know a shy and introverted priest on the East Coast whose vision and spirituality and sincerity draw people to him in such numbers and with such commitment that the parish community lives the Sermon on the Mount in a way that far surpasses what one could imagine for a community that size.

The same is true for laity and religious in leadership. The DRE of one parish described a woman who volunteered to bake cookies for the catechists. She wanted to contribute something but felt she didn't have what was needed to do anything more than that. Over time the DRE recognized extraordinary abilities in this person and created opportunities that encouraged her growth. This person eventually attained a master's degree in religious education and today leads a group of catechists in a highly creative program.

In your own life, you have no doubt known many leaders—perhaps a teacher or a catechist, perhaps a cleric or a religious or a layperson. This person may have been a classmate, a friend, or a fellow committee member.

Name two or three people you would call "leader." Why do you call them "leader"?

1. _____

2. _____

3. _____

As these people look to Jesus as their model, and indeed as you yourself do the same, what kind of leadership qualities might you find? Jesus left no doubt about the style of his leadership when he said, "For the Son of Man came not to be served, but to serve" (Mk 10:45). This is how Jesus described his style of leadership—that of a servant. In reading the accounts of his relationships with others, we cannot avoid noticing how Jesus consistently put himself at the service of others. He consoled his friends at the loss of a loved one; he taught on a frequent basis, giving new ideas and inspiration and courage; he healed in many different ways—physically, spiritually, relationally; he prayed for others. Jesus also served by feeding his followers food of all kinds, including and perhaps especially hope, by describing a vision of what could be. He led and served by encouraging and shaping future leaders. In other words, he served. Jesus was the servant-leader.

Servant leadership, the term coined and preached by Robert Greenleaf, was made popular in his 1977 book of the same title (Paulist Press, 1991). Although Greenleaf, who died in 1990, was a Quaker, he was first a long-time leader in business and industry. Much later he became a true wisdom figure and a powerful voice in shaping leaders in religious and nonprofit groups. His simple and profound premise was like that of Jesus': that in order to be an effective leader anywhere, in any circumstances, one must become a servant to those being led.

"The real test of the leader," Greenleaf wrote, "is whether those served grow as persons. Do they become healthier, wiser, freer, more likely themselves to become servants?" Greenleaf is clear that true leadership, effective leadership, must begin with the inclination that one wants to serve, even "to serve *first*," he says. Thus, the basis and heart and motivation of a leader is not egocentric or the desire for power. In fact, the desire for power and authority is suspect, because it is the antithesis of leadership.

In a way, servant leadership is akin to Thomas Aquinas's description of love as wanting to bring about what is good for the beloved.

Greenleaf goes on to confidently state that "among the legions of deprived and unsophisticated people are many true servants who will lead. Most of them can also learn to discriminate among those who presume to serve them and identify the true servants whom they will follow." It is for this reason, he believes, that people will respond freely only to those leaders who are proven and trusted servants.

True leaders are followed voluntarily. Both the introvert and the extrovert described above had only voluntary followers. Although people do follow, at times, out of coercion or fear or duty, "followership" freely given is the highest form and is certainly what the disciples of Jesus had. Jesus never coerced or threatened; rather, he invited—and his servanthood, his message, and his vision attracted others. Why would we want anything less in our community than leaders who are followed voluntarily?

So we look at our leader, Jesus, to see how we are to lead. We reflect on his qualities that we want to emulate if we are to lead successfully. Loughlan Sofield and Donald Kuhl give us some specific help in this task of reflecting on Jesus' qualities in their book, *The Collaborative Leader* (Ave Maria Press, 1995). In writing their book, these authors interviewed forty-two outstanding Christians who are noted leaders in their respective professional fields—education, business, medicine, politics, and others. These people, the authors explain, emulate the very leadership qualities of Jesus.

Sofield and Kuhl describe Jesus, the model for Christian leaders, as leading through these qualities: listening and responding to others; creating a vision; being authentic and compassionate; forgiving others; being straightforward and generative; being inclusive, especially of those who are alienated and marginalized; empowering others; and, significantly, being a person of integrity.

Listening and Responding to Others

True listening in an adult-to-adult exchange or a dialogue setting that gives the leader access to the people as well as an understanding of their needs. When a leader is in touch with what others are saying, he or she learns what is needed by the community—whether it is a group volunteering on a project, a parish committee or council, or an entire diocese. Whatever its role, the group will be effective to the extent that it has what it needs for the task. Perhaps what it needs is more of a community connection with one another; perhaps more spiritual resources, such as better homilies or faith formation; perhaps the group needs something as simple as a place to do its work or materials and supplies for its volunteer ministry. Whatever its needs, large or small, a group needs to speak and the leader needs to hear and respond. Listening well reveals the state of the community—and it is essential for the leader to know how to listen well. Listening well means listening first with the ears but also with the heart, intuition, experience, and vision that the leader brings in order to hear the unspoken, perhaps not-yet-conscious needs of the group.

"That which is received is received according to the mode of the recipient." In this bit of wisdom, Saint Thomas Aquinas points out that it is essential for the leader to listen well in order to find out where the people are and then to "go there" to meet them as a starting point for a new vision. A good listener has a relationship with the group, and *relationship* is at the heart of leadership. As Max DePree points out in *Leadership Is an Art* (Dell Publishing, 1989), "Leadership is more tribal than scientific, more a weaving of relationships than an amassing of information." Nowhere is this more important than in a Christian community which, if we follow the challenge and message of Jesus, is primarily about connecting with others, about relationships, about caring for others.

Leaders clearly need big ears. The prayer of Saint Francis of Assisi asks, "Lord, grant that I may not so much seek to be understood as to understand." This is a very time-consuming dimension of the servant-leader and one that the leader must deeply believe in lest the urgent tasks of the day obscure this important dimension of leadership. The good leader, we must realize, needs to understand the followers much more than the followers need to understand the leader.

Creating a Vision

The leader helps the community articulate and commit to its vision. Clearly, one of the reasons people found Jesus attractive—and still do today—is that his message struck a familiar chord, a longing, or a sense of what *should* be that is in the listeners' hearts. This response often is something they may have only felt but not even articulated before. But here, in Jesus, is someone who speaks what is in the hearts of others and gives them hope about it and points them toward a way of making it happen. This hope generates energy and commitment to move ahead toward a common good. The servant-leader doesn't need to have all the ideas, but he or she can listen well and help the group articulate what it may already know intuitively. Again, Max DePree says it well: "The first responsibility of a leader is to define reality. The last is to say thank you. In between the two, the leader must become a servant and a debtor." In defining reality, the leader speaks over and over again of the mission and of the way(s) that mission can be more fully lived out in this time and place. DePree refers to the leader in this capacity as a "tribal storyteller." Jesus painted a picture of how people could live and what life, this one and the next, could be. He shared his vision of God's loving care for all people and, indeed, for all the created world. Jesus spoke over and over again of how this vision could change things for his followers and what was expected of them if they chose to be a part of it. As the saying goes, "Unhappy is a people that has run out of words to describe what is happening to them." Servant-leaders find the words.

Being Authentic and Compassionate

Jesus gave us the model of a leader who is aware of the concerns, problems, and even sufferings of his or her followers. He genuinely cared about his followers' well-being and problems. Jesus displayed his compassion authentically and openly. He cried with those who suffered, listened to people's concerns even if trivial, held the hands of those who needed healing, and offered genuine consolation to the bereaved. This kind of true compassion cannot be forced or pretended. In fact, it is only compassion when it is authentic.

Forgiving

The image of Peter publicly denying Jesus three times and of the resurrected Christ's subsequent appearance to him and charging him to carry on after the Ascension stands out as a model for forgiveness. The leader who harbors grudges, who lets the past be an obstacle to carrying out the mission today, is not a true leader. Inevitably, community experiences— working together and meeting together and planning, and executing together—lead to conflict and hurts and misunderstandings. Like Jesus, the leader needs to have a forgiving heart so that the work, the mission of Christ, can be accomplished.

Being Straightforward and Generative

Clarity and commitment are often mentioned as the two significant qualities for a group to work well together. It is up to the leader to model these in dealing with staff and volunteers. Clarity about the mission and the tasks, clarity about expectations, and clarity that results from getting rid of unspoken assumptions all contribute to effective ministry together. Religious groups tend to be strong on commitment but not so strong on clarity. Yet, the two go hand in hand. Commitment is actually generated by a clear understanding of the mission and goals. Commitment is fostered by the successful work that comes from being clear about what the job is and what the expectations are.

Including All

Preferring to be with certain people more than with others is part of human nature. It is only natural, therefore, to have a preference toward people like ourselves or who agree with us or think like we do. But this is obviously neither the nature of a parish community nor a quality of Christian behavior. Jesus certainly gave us many examples of associating with various types of people; he turned away no one. Rather, he spoke with community leaders and ate with sinners. In fact, he made a point, it would seem from the stories in the gospels, of particularly including those whom the world would not: prostitutes, reviled tax collectors, the lame and the blind, the "little ones" of all kinds. And today, they (perhaps we) exist in every parish. One teacher referred to them as the "door people"—those on the fringes, those whom we do not even see because they are hanging back by the door rather than placing themselves in the center of the community, in the midst of activity. Leaders find such people and model inclusion of them for the rest of the parish.

I am reminded of Steven, who came to many parish activities by himself. He would smile at people and nod, but he always hung back from participating. Even in small groups at faith formation events, he would appear interested but have nothing to say, even in his small group. Steven was a wise and well-educated person, but he was extremely self-conscious of his stutter. It was only when Cathy, one of the small-group leaders, took the time to draw him out patiently and respectfully, that Steven began to share what he had to offer. Others, too, began to take the initiative with him, talking with him informally and, in a short time, he became comfortable in joining with the group by offering his own insights. Steven was no longer a door person. And Cathy had tears in her eyes the day she received a lovely note from Steven thanking her for her kindness to him. Both of their lives had been enriched.

Empowering Others

The servant-leader who follows Jesus actively supports the gifts and ministry of others. He or she does not cling tightly to power and authority, but rather multiplies service by developing and even challenging others to use their own gifts. Regarding aspects of their own roles, good leaders constantly ask, "Who else can do this?" And they continually call forth those persons with the talent to do the task. This is what good teachers do also. Good teachers know what they don't know, trust in the group, and see the potential in others and call it forth.

Many years ago I was scheduled to conduct a workshop at a college in California. Although I was the leader of the course, I knew that there would be much talent, experience, and knowledge within the group. Although that was no great insight, I also knew that the configuration of the furniture in the room could both teach that principle and enable the exchange of ideas to happen more easily. Thus, the morning of the first day of the workshop, I arrived early and arranged the chairs from rows into a circle. As the group members began to gather, I stood out in the hallway to greet them as they entered the room. Finally, when all were present, I walked back into the room only to find that the chairs had been rearranged, positioned back into neat rows, and leaving everyone facing the front of the room. Of course, I proceeded to invite the group to shuffle the chairs back into a circle and then to explore the assumptions that had led the group to pull apart the circle configuration and organize the chairs in rows. While teaching and leading may be separate roles, I know that, as John Gardner says, "Every great leader is clearly teaching and every great teacher is leading."

Being a Person of Integrity

The true test of being Christian lies in how we grow in integrating what we say we believe with what we do and who we are. As a young classroom teacher, I kept a sign facing me on my desk. It contained the old adage that read: "What you are shouts so loudly that I cannot hear what you say." Credibility is inevitably connected with integrity. No matter where we live and work, we are always evangelizing by the way we live our lives and how we treat others. For the servant-leader to have credibility and the honor of leadership, this self-awareness is critical. Part of our life journey is regularly taking time to assess how we're doing, how we did this very day, in integrating what we say we believe with how we behave with others. Obviously, none of us is fully there yet, but the question is, How diligently am I working toward this integrity that, for most of us, will be fully realized only in the next life?

The leader of volunteers in a parish I visited cared for her volunteers the way she hoped they cared for those they served. She got to know people personally and took time to listen to their stories. She knew what they hoped to get from their volunteering, helped them find just the right place to use their skills in rewarding ways, challenged them with new goals, and treated them with professional respect. She listened to the tales of their family life, remembered their birthdays, affirmed them with compliments, and bragged about them to others in their presence. She told the rest of the parish community about their service and organized the annual Celebration of Caring Dinner, in honor of the volunteers' selfless service to the parish. In a word, this woman acted with integrity. This kind of behavior, she knew, must be sincere to be authentic and credible. Her only problem was that the culture of care and community she created among the parish volunteers was so attractive that she had more volunteers than she could use! This is a problem many parish leaders would love to have—and it was a tribute to this woman's leadership ability. It is a problem we can all have!

Here are some questions that will help you reflect on the qualities and skills of leaders:

- Write the names of two or three leaders you know/have known that you consider successful.

- What qualities do/did these people exhibit that cause you to consider them leaders?

- What are the three qualities of a servant-leader you would like to develop further in yourself?

- Write that desire into a goal for yourself:
  I would like to…

- Who or what will help you put this goal into action?

Resources for Additional Reading

DePree, Max. *Leadership Is an Art.* New York: Dell Publishing, 1989.

Fraker, Anne T., and Larry C. Spears, eds. *The Private Writings of Robert K. Greenleaf—Seeker and Servant: Reflections on Religious Leadership.* San Francisco: Jossey-Bass, Inc., 1996.

Gardner, John W. *On Leadership.* New York: The Free Press, 1990.

Greenleaf, Robert K. *Servant Leadership: A Journey Into the Nature of Legitimate Power and Greatness.* Mahwah, N.J.: Paulist Press, 1977.

Sofield, Loughlan and Donald Kuhn, *The Collaborative Leader.* Notre Dame, IN: Ave Maria Press, 1995.

CHAPTER 2

The Person of the Leader: What Is Inside

~

The real test of the leader is whether those served grow as persons. Do they become healthier, wiser, freer, more like themselves to become servants?

ROBERT GREENLEAF

Not long ago, I visited a large bookstore that is part of a national chain. As I passed through the business section on my way to the coffee shop, a title on the spine of one of the books caught my eye. *Soul,* it said. Thinking I had misread what section I was in, I stopped. No, this title was, indeed, a business book. Curious, I began reading through the other titles. *Truly,* I thought, *one might wonder if this were the religion section rather than the business section.* Words such as *spirituality, mission, heart, purpose,* and yes, even *soul* seemed to be everywhere. It appears that the secular world has finally peeked into the religious world and made this discovery: it is what is inside a person, the values and beliefs that people hold, which affect what kind of people they are, how they behave, and what kind of leader they are able to be.

Those who lead in parishes and religious organizations smile at such an epiphany by secular writers, business gurus who write that we must "lead with soul"; we must "have a journey of the spirit"; we must "care about each other"; and we must "have a purposeful dream" if we want our enterprise to do well, our people to flourish. And while these authors are right, we've known this for centuries.

In parish leadership, wisdom such as this is assumed. *Of course,* our beliefs affect who we are. *Of course*, what we do is faith-based—and, indeed, was so even before the government coopted the term. *Of course*, we have must have clear values and beliefs and gospel motivation. *Of course*, our vision should be grounded in spirituality and we must know how to treat one another with dignity.

However, those of us in leadership roles today need to challenge ourselves and ask: Is this really always true in our parish? Are there times when it may be true more in theory than in practice? Do we always lead with soul? Do your leaders always have a conscious and purposeful dream? Are we always on a journey of the spirit?

Joanne had been in parish ministry for fourteen years. She had had filled many roles, from part-time volunteer to full-time paid staff member. But now she felt she needed out. She no longer had the passion and commitment she once had, and parishioners seemed rather indifferent, less friendly. None but the most committed seemed to heed her calls for volunteers or even seemed interested in offering ideas. She was working long hours with little satisfaction and seemed either on autopilot or unsure about where her projects and ministries were headed.

Fortunately for Joanne, her conversations with her spiritual director enabled her to recognize that her initial fire and motivation about ministry and service had moved to the back burner. The clarity she once had about the mission of her ministry had become cobwebbed and beyond her daily awareness, due perhaps in part to the pace of her schedule and the demands on her time. The vision of what she wanted to accomplish had become dimmed and so had the underlying spiritual motivation.

Joanne knew she had been a different kind of leader in ministry when she had that clear vision about her mission. It wasn't so much that she needed a new career or even a sabbatical. But it was clear that she needed to do some reflection. She began to do the work necessary to discover her own personal mission and to connect that mission with her ministry. Before long, Joanne found her energy increased, and, over a period of weeks and months, people began to respond positively again. She focused on fewer major projects at once. Even her prayer life seemed to come out of a long period of darkness. As a result of this reflection, Joanne learned some important lessons, not the least of which was to keep her eye on the ball, to thank God for the gifts she's been given, to recall and pray over her mission daily, and to consciously use her talents on behalf of the mission which God had given her to accomplish on this earth.

Joanne had been so busy with external details that she had forgotten to nurture her own spiritual life. She fit the astute comment of Saint Augustine who said, "People travel to wonder at the height of mountains, and they pass by themselves without wondering."

Personal Mission

Talking about "personal mission" may sound as trendy as the titles of recent business books mentioned previously. Nevertheless, for the Christian leader to be most effective, personal mission is essential. While it is said that every person has a mission, those who are clear about their own mission can use it as a tool to be focused, to integrate the parts of their life. People with clear personal missions are able to realize energy and satisfaction from life and to keep failures in perspective and learn from them.

In working with Kaleel Jamison on her book about leadership, self-empowerment, and personal growth (*The Nibble Theory and the Kernel of Power*, Paulist Press, 1984), I vividly recall her saying that she never made mistakes in her decisions because she knew what she was here for. At the time, I had a mixture of something like mild annoyance and confusion. Perhaps it was even jealousy and longing for that same peace, that same certitude. But as I got to know Kaleel and appreciate her beliefs in personal mission, I understood the plain truth of what she wrote: "For my part, I *do* believe that I have come to this world for a mission—for some specific reason. And that doesn't mean that I have to bring peace to the Middle East—although I yearn to do so. I don't have to be Madame Curie. Or Albert Schweitzer. But I *can* do certain things to touch certain people on this earth—in this life, my life. I can make myself grow in such a way that it affects both me and others. I am worthwhile. And so, I believe, are you….It is part of the great paradox that when you discover that Self—your kernel—you are likely to know fully why you're here, how you fit in, how you're part of the great universal human community."

But how does one go about defining a personal mission and then making decisions to live by it?

Many people have described and written about ways to name or discover one's personal mission. The process Kaleel described in detail is simply put: spend time thinking, journaling, or talking with a confidant about basic questions:

- What things give me joy or are important to me?

- Why are each of these things important to me?

- What things do I do well?

- Which of these things are not learned but rather are innate gifts or qualities?

- From this examination, what are the patterns or themes that emerge that describe me most accurately?

Kaleel insists that if we are to discover why we are on this earth and what our personal mission is, we will need to take time with this process. She believed that if one is honest and patient with the process as it develops, you will be able to discover why you are on this earth and what your personal mission is. Before she died, Kaleel was dedicated to coaching people along this path. From experience, she and the people she mentored knew the benefits and rewards of such clarity from experience.

Others, such as Steven Covey, recommend taking several months to create a personal mission statement. Covey suggests choosing three days during upcoming months to spend a half an hour each day working on your statement. He, too, describes the mission statement as capturing your unique purpose in life and naming the qualities you want to develop or the accomplishments to which you aspire. This, he believes, becomes a beacon or guide to help you fulfill your life vision. It inspires you and enables you to make life-decisions with greater ease and confidence. Covey suggests asking yourself questions such as:

- Who have been major positive influences in my life and how have I been influenced by them?

- What are some of my talents and positive qualities?

- What would I like to contribute with my life?

- How do I wish people would describe me?

Other people who are life-mission coaches suggest writing your own ideal obituary or imagining what you would like others to say about you when you leave the room. A friend of mine shudders at such questions.

She prefers to approach the task by writing a press release describing what she has hopefully accomplished or what she wanted to accomplish, as though it has already happened.

Some spiritual directors suggest a simple journaling method of writing a few paragraphs responding to the following starter phrase:

I will have lived a successful life if....

Whatever method of clarification we choose for naming our own personal life mission, it is a step toward discerning God's will in our lives. For we know, as Thomas Aquinas said, "Grace builds on nature." Honoring our nature, our God-given talents and skills in a role that uses them, must be doing God's will. That is not to say there is only one job, one path, one ministry, for each of us. But the goal is congruence between our mission and our ministry or work. After all, our life's work is bigger than our job, our work, or our ministry. Our life's work should direct and determine what it is that we do. Work or ministry is a piece of life and should help fulfill life's purpose, not vice versa.

True leadership is rooted in leading your life in a conscious, purposeful way. Acquiring this conscious purpose requires a serious commitment of time to this kind of ongoing personal reflection. When you start with personal leadership, you soon find many ways to influence and lead others beyond yourself. Taking time to reflect, to meditate on your mission, keeps you grounded in the gospel motivation. Because you've discovered this correlation between your personal mission and your religious beliefs, you have found a way to combine, correlate, and strengthen the two. And what a blessing it is to achieve even a partial personal integration!

A Genuine Life

Some coaching clients say that once they have this clarity of purpose, they feel they are living life rather than just passing through it. It is not just great leaders such as Martin Luther King, Jr., who are able to say "I have a dream." Rather, all those who are grounded in self-understanding have a richer, more meaningful life because they know what God wants of them, because they are clear about why they are here. What a liberating and energizing experience that is.

Lee G. Bolman in his book *Leading With Soul* reminds us that leading is giving. But it is not so much the giving of *things* or the giving of *ideas* as it is the giving of *oneself*—not just giving one's time, but the real treasure of giving of oneself. And an awareness of what that treasure is allows the gift to be given fully and deliberately.

Mark was between jobs and was flattered by the call from a head hunter. Following their phone conversation, he sent a résumé, because the position sounded exciting. The following week, he was thrilled when he was invited to fly to the coast for an interview. After preparing carefully, practicing what he would say, and even role-playing the upcoming interview with the help of a friend, Mark thought he would do well— and he did. Afterwards, confident he would be given an offer, he rented a car to drive around the city, and even planned to check out housing possibilities the next day.

The following morning, however, Mark found himself delaying the housing search. Trying to sort out his hesitation, he went for a long walk, sat on a park bench, and reviewed all the good things about the new challenge, were it offered to him: wonderful people, a great salary and benefits, a prestigious position. But from somewhere inside, the words formed and actually came out of his mouth: "This is not really me. This is not how I want to spend my life." He looked around, chagrined. Mark's surprise at the words was only outdone by the great feeling of relief he suddenly had experienced. It was a moment of liberation. Now, years later, and in a role where he is using his talents and experiencing fulfillment in what he does, Mark has no regrets—only a kind of amazement at his own clarity and courage. "Now I'm following my own life mission," he says. "The money would have been great, but happiness and fulfillment come from being true to yourself."

How fortunate for Mark to have learned this lesson at an early age: Be true to yourself. For most of us, gaining this wisdom requires us to take the time and effort to discover ourselves. Time and commitment and sometimes hard work are what bring us to the place where Mark found himself—and it's worth the effort. Bolman notes, "The heart of leadership is in the hearts of leaders. You have to lead from something deep in your heart."

1. Choose one of the methods described above, or a different one, and commit to spending time with yourself and with the process.

2. When will you work on your journey inward to write your mission statement?

3. With whom might you share this process?

4. Name several ways in which you will you use your personal statement when it is completed?

True leadership grows out of integrity and a grounded sense of your own concerns and needs; it starts when you begin to lead yourself in a purposeful way. When you are clear about who you are and where you want to go, this reflective self-examination becomes a way of life. Leading yourself successfully is the first requirement for leading others. What is your agenda for you?

In desiring to become a leader or in striving to be a better leader, the primary motivation should be the inner satisfaction that comes from giving of yourself. This giving can be directed to an individual, a group, or an entire parish—all for the purpose of helping others create their own competence, their own commitment. It is not the size of the accomplishment that makes you an effective leader. Rather, it is the creating of something worthwhile and lasting in this world. This is what a servant-leader is; this is what a servant-leader does.

Resources for Additional Reading

Bolman, Lee G., and Terrence E. Deal. *Leading With Soul: An Uncommon Journey of Spirit.* San Francisco: Jossey-Bass, Inc., 1995.

Covey, Stephen. *The 7 Habits of Highly Effective People.* New York: Simon and Schuster, 1990.

Hudson, Frederic M., and Pamela D. McLean. *Life Launch: A Passionate Guide to the Rest of Your Life.* Santa Barbara, CA: The Hudson Institute, 1995.

Jamison, Kaleel. *The Nibble Theory and the Kernel of Power: A Book About Leadership, Self-Empowerment, and Personal Growth.* Ramsey, N.J.: Paulist Press, 1984.

Sofield, Loughlan, and Donald H. Kuhn. *The Collaborative Leader: Listening to the Wisdom of God's People.* Notre Dame, IN: Ave Maria Press, 1995.

Sweetser, Thomas, and Carol Holden. *Leadership in a Successful Parish.* Kansas City, MO: Sheed & Ward, 1992.

Whitehead, James D., and Evelyn Eaton Whitehead. *The Promise of Partnership: Leadership and Ministry in an Adult Church.* San Francisco: HarperCollins Publishers, 1991.

CHAPTER 3

Planning Together: Bringing About the Kingdom of God

~

If you don't know where you're going, how will you know if you get there?

AN OLD SAYING

W hen I visit parishes around the country, I like to try to get a feel for the parish by visiting the worship space and looking through whatever materials are available in the back of the church. These things say a lot about the community even before meeting the people.

Once, when I was visiting St. Martin's, a medium-sized parish in the Midwest, I encountered a rather remarkable church building. It was constructed after the Second Vatican Council, with a design that was simple, warm, and awe-inspiring. It was not the architecture, however, that most caught my interest. Rather, I was quite taken by, of all things, the parish calendar: it was everywhere. In the gathering space of the church there was a large wall covered with a changeable calendar displaying the liturgical season and the parish activities for the current month and the upcoming months. Special liturgical events such as first Communion were indicated. Though it was quite large, the calendar was simply done, and not out of place in the tasteful space where it had been positioned. I then noticed that the calendar for the current month was displayed on the back cover of the weekly bulletin, but done with more detail. Also available in the back of the church was a parish booklet listing the names of all the parish organizations and volunteer opportunities and, yes, the calendar—this one for the whole year, in a form somewhat abbreviated from the bulletin. The parish calendar was indeed a mechanism for telling parishioners "who's on first."

Later, in talking with the pastoral council, I mentioned the high visibility of the parish calendar. The council members were so enthusiastic about the surprising effects the public calendar had on the community. Initially, they explained, the annual calendar was a planning tool for the council and staff. Over time, however, it grew and blossomed into a reliable vehicle of communication, consciousness raising, motivation, and even community building. Not only were parishioners happy to see what was happening beyond their own circles of involvement, but everyone, including the council, was quite amazed at how much activity was happening when it was all seen together at a glance.

As a result of the wide posting of the calendar, many people in this parish discovered ministry opportunities, classes, social activities, and prayer and worship gatherings in which they were interested and in which they wanted to participate. Projects grew as more people got involved. Parishioners began to meet new people as a result, and, as these connections deepened, so did the spirit of community and caring. The staff also found the calendar helpful in managing the space needs and negotiating schedules when there were possible conflicts. There were now no surprises as sometimes happened when two groups showed up to use a space at the same time!

As time passed, the uses for the calendar grew. Seeing a kind of overview snapshot helped the council look at what was being done, what wasn't being done, and what the parish priorities looked like. With this clear vision, the council was able to take beginning steps down the path of pastoral planning.

A parish calendar is a simple and basic tool. Beyond seeing "who's on first base," it gives a vision of who we are and what we do. It can provide a shocking picture of how well we're living up to who we say we are as a church and as a people of God. We are told that our values are reflected in how we spend our money. It is likewise true that how we spend our time is a major indicator of our values, in both our personal life and our community life. The calendar is like looking in a mirror that says, "Here you are. This is what you look like." Then, of course, we must ask whether this is who we want to be and, if not, what we want to change.

And that's just what happened at St. Martin's. After the council and the pastor discussed all that the calendar indicated the parish was doing, they were ready to ask: "What *should* we be doing?"

"We need a plan," they eventually agreed, and over time, the pastor and the parish pastoral council began to formulate what was needed to involve the parish in planning for the future—and this discussion led to the question of the parish mission statement. Although someone seemed to recall that there was one someplace, the mission statement obviously was not being used as either a guide or an evaluation touchstone. So the pastor and the council committed to the task of revisiting the parish mission statement as the first key step in the pastoral planning process.

Every parish has a mission, whether or not it has a formal mission "statement." The mission of the Church, of course, is to continue the mission of Christ. The Church does not exist for itself. Rather, it exists for the mission of Jesus, to continue his work in our corner of the world at this moment in history. It exists to bring about the kingdom of God through Word, Worship, Service, and Community. These are the means we use to effect the mission; they are not ends in themselves.

Word

We are people of the Word. We proclaim and hear the Word in faith-formation gatherings and in various other kinds of teaching and formation experiences. For example, we proclaim the Word in our sacramental preparations: in our offerings of RCIA or infant baptism preparation to marriage preparation. We proclaim the Word in all the dimensions of our Catholic schools, and to children and youth who participate in our parish catechetical classes. Our intergenerational programs, adult faith formation offerings, and small groups that do Scripture study are all occasions of proclaiming the Word.

We know, however, that the brief homily at Sunday Mass is all the formation most Catholics receive. The Sunday Scripture readings and the homily provide what we take with us to our homes and workplace for the rest of the week. They are our guidance and spiritual nourishment for the week's journey as disciples of Christ, The homily, like the Scriptures themselves, offers both comfort and challenge. They give us both encouragement and hope. They also challenge us to examine our lifestyle, the way we act in our day-to-day activities and relationships. They confront us with the sharp edge of the two-edged sword of the Scriptures. In order to both comfort and challenge, the homily and the Scriptures must connect with our life, with the real world that most people live in day to day. This is the only way the Word can leave church after the Sunday liturgy and make a difference. Only when we take the Word into our lives on Monday through Saturday are we proclaiming the Word outside of the community and evangelizing through our lives. And this, we know, is the most effective avenue of evangelization. Proclamation of the Word is integral to our parish mission. Here are some very crucial questions regarding proclamation of the Word of God in your parish.

- What are the various ways your parish proclaims the Word of God? List as many as you can.

- Does the parish staff reflect together on the Sunday readings to help the priest connect the lives of parishioners with the Scripture message in each Sunday's homily? How else can the priest be supported in this critical ministry of connecting life and Word?

- Where else in your parish does the Word get proclaimed?

- How effectively is the Word proclaimed in the parish's formation and catechetical programs? What specific groups of people do these programs touch?

- As you look at the list that you formulated detailing the ways in which your parish proclaims the Word of God, who in the parish are you neglecting in this regard? What special interests or age groups are not included and why? What can be done about this neglect?

- How do you train and support your catechetical leaders? What challenges do you face in the training and support of your catechetical leaders, and who can help address those challenges?

- How do you continue the formation of your leaders, staff, and volunteers through periodicals, workshops, classes, and so on, so that they continue to be spiritually nurtured and challenged?

- What other concerns do you need to address with regard to proclaiming the Word and hearing the Word?

Worship

We worship, particularly through the Eucharist, the "source and sum-mit" of our lives. We come to Sunday liturgy to be spiritually fed and strengthened so that we might live better lives "in the world." Likewise, we also come to bring the fruits of our lives—our actions, our living of the gospel, our relationships, our successes and failures—and to offer them to God at Mass. We participate in worship when we celebrate each of the sacraments as a community. Here we are sharing and sanctifying important moments and passages in our lives. The worship and prayer in a parish is the heart of the parish community—and the Eucharist is our highest and most important form of worship.

We also know that Jesus told us to pray always: pray through the year in the liturgical seasons; pray through the week as we go about our lives; pray through the day as we meet life's joys and challenges, and respond; pray always and pray all ways. What's more, we need different kinds of prayer at different ages in our life and different kinds of prayer for differ-ent moments along our journey of faith.

Jesus gave us a model of someone who prayed all ways. For example, Jesus prayed formal community prayer and ritual prayer at the Last Sup-per. He did this also with his community in the local synagogue. We know he prayed the Psalms and he participated in the study of Scripture. We know, too, that he had many times of private, individual prayer: he prayed alone in the Garden of Gethsemane as his friends slept; he went on re-treat to the desert, especially before beginning his public life; and he also escaped the crowds to be alone in prayer. Jesus prayed spontaneous prayer, such as on the cross when he prayed for those crucifying him and for those crucified with him. In other words, Jesus prayed always and he prayed in many different styles. We, too, need a broad repertoire of prayer styles to meet our needs at different times in our lives.

When I was driving through the ice and sleet to catch a plane to get to my hospitalized daughter, I could only grip the steering wheel and pray, "O God, be with me!"

In the quiet moments of an early morning, we might want to hold the rosary and pray its familiar repetitions.

In the joy of seeing a newborn baby, we might want to sing a psalm.

After my friend's spouse died, he told the pastor he could no longer pray. The wise priest responded, "That's what we're here for…to pray for you until you are able to pray yourself."

When a Lenten group gathers in someone's living room, it might pray the Scriptures together.

I visited a parish in Michigan and stood in the sunny schoolyard when the recess bell rang and a small red-haired boy burst out the door, raced across the blacktop, threw up his arms, lifted his face to the sun, and exclaimed, "Praise the Lord for this beautiful day!"

We may need to chant simply and quietly in our community reconciliation service. On another occasion, we might "pray and sway" as we are caught up in the rhythm of a loud hymn.

Some pray with mariachis and others with drums.

Like Jesus, we need different kinds of prayer at different times. That requires that we have the full treasure chest of our tradition to dip into— a treasure chest that includes the following:

- Sunday liturgies that are celebrated with the full and active participation of parishioners, with liturgical ministers who are well trained and liturgical music that enables the community to participate;

- liturgical art that is inspiring and exhibits a simple nobility;

- sacramental celebrations that are true expressions of the life of the parish, including Liturgy of the Word with children;

- devotional prayer that is theologically solid and in proportion to the primary place of the sacraments;

- experiences such as Liturgy of the Hours and guided meditation, to broaden our experiences and taste the ancient traditions of the Church.

Here are some questions that might be useful in evaluating the prayer life of your parish.

- How do you support your community in its prayer life?

- What kinds of opportunities are available for community prayer?

- How do you support and encourage a variety of prayer styles?

• What kinds of aids and encouragement are provided for helping people continue prayer during the week? Are the Scripture readings for each day of the week listed in the bulletin so that individuals can reflect on them each day?

• How are people in the community informed of who is sick or alone and needs daily prayer? Who takes Communion regularly to those who are housebound or ill?

• How do you encourage families to pray together, especially during Lent and Advent?

• What else might we consider doing to foster prayer life in the parish community? How can you find out what people need to feel supported and nurtured in their prayer life?

• Is prayer is a keystone of your parish mission?

Service

Christians are called to serve. Thus, we are the Church continuing the mission of Christ only when we are servants. Jesus taught us by word and action that service is central to the identity of a Christian. And so, as a community, we strive to be of service, meeting the needs of our community members and looking outward to the neighborhood, to the diocese, to the country, and indeed, to the needs of our brothers and sisters throughout the world. We look for ways to be healers of pain of all kinds and to be voices for the voiceless. When we do this, we are discovering how to live the beatitudes in our own day and age. For we know as a community that Jesus was speaking to us today when he said, "What you did to the least of these, you did to me."

There are many ways to live as a community of service. For example, a serving parish might organize a program of instruction, adaptable for all ages, in social teaching from the encyclicals, gospels, and letters of the bishops, to help raise awareness of our call and motivate parishioners to gospel-based action. A serving parish might participate in local, national, and international helping efforts, encouraging parishioners to engage in these efforts outside of the faith community as well. A serving parish networks with other parishes and denominations, as well as with social agencies, to assist the unemployed, the hungry, and the homeless. A servant people integrates serving into every aspect of their parish life. A serving parish does not leave its efforts in this regard to a "social action committee." Rather, the call to service is directed to each person and each community. This call includes the charge to both educate to that call and provide the means to carry it out. It should be clear to all parishioners that a community in service is a community continuing the mission of Jesus and the Church.

Community

Members of the early church communities were known by their loving lifestyle: "See how they love one another," said observers of Christian behavior. Today, community remains at the heart of our mission and Christian identity. But community doesn't just magically happen. Rather, the building of community needs to be consciously and continuously developed in many formal and informal ways. Community building is how the members of the Body of Christ connect with one another in meaningful ways.

Experience has taught us an important corollary: community is not only a goal but is also the fruit of our efforts. It is the result of hearing the Word, worshiping well together, and "doing" service together. All these efforts bring about community. When we learn together and are formed together in our faith, when we share Eucharist and the sacraments, when we work together to bring about peace and justice and feed the hungry, we become more deeply connected to one another—and a more deeply bonded community results. Sociologists tell us that a community focused only on itself is doomed to failure.

There are many ways we experience community within the parish. And there are innumerable ways to foster, encourage, and allow community to develop. A sense of community cannot be forced or artificially created; however, parish leaders have a major role in encouraging and cultivating community within a parish family. (We explore this further in chapter four.)

Although every parish forms a particular community, each and every parish has the same mission because the parish is where the Church actually lives. While we may think of the Church as living at the Vatican or at the diocesan chancery, the life, not the administration and leadership, actually occurs in parish after parish after parish.

Despite this commonality, each parish mission is unique because each community has unique characteristics, a unique culture, and a unique history. How this particular parish began and continues today, what the surrounding culture needs from it, what the makeup of the people is, and many other factors shape each parish's mission statement differently. The tiny church far up into the remote hills of a village of Jamaica, the military parish on a U.S. Army base in Europe, the affluent suburban parish in Ohio, the city parish in the Philippines, the multi-cultural urban parish in San Francisco—all these share in the same mission of Christ and yet will reflect their differences in their mission statements.

Crafting the Mission Statement

The creation of a parish mission statement is a serious process and must involve as many people as possible. The following scenario follows St. Martin's parish in the development of its mission statement through three essential phases: listening to the parish; drafting a mission statement and presenting it to the community; and integrating the mission statement into various ministries.

Listening to the Parish

When the pastoral council at St. Martin's decided to develop a parish mission statement, it began by holding a series of listening sessions in the parish. It invited parishioners to reflect together on their vision of the parish and what it meant to them. As these parish groups met, a group of people were asked to record their main ideas so that they could craft a statement that would reflect the entire community. Once the dates for the listening sessions were set, parishioners were notified of these dates—by way of announcements in the bulletin and after Mass, through their inclusion in the parish calendar, and the posting of information broadsides throughout the church facilities—over the course of two weeks prior to the dates. The Sunday morning sessions were held between Masses, coffee and donuts were provided, and the pastor welcomed those attending.

Then the facilitator explained the process of creating (or revising) a parish mission statement:

- The first step is to *listen* to the people in the parish.

- Next the council will *reflect* on what comes out of the listening sessions.

- A writing team will then *create* a draft that the council will critique and possibly modify.

- The mission statement will be *presented* to the parish for ratification at the Sunday liturgies.

- Finally, the mission statement will be *used* by the council in doing pastoral planning, by the staff in connecting all ministry efforts to the mission, by each group in the parish in understanding how they are connected to the larger work of all other parish activities.

Next, the facilitator reviewed for the group the purpose of a parish mission statement:

- The mission statement defines for us *why* our parish exists.

- The mission statement states what effect it will have because of its existence. How will it put its gifts at the service of the local Church and the universal Church?

- The mission statement clarifies the identity of the parish.

- The mission statement sets a general direction for what the parish is here to do, so that planning can take place based on the mission of the parish. This is the tool that parish leadership and administration will use as a basis for decisions.

- The mission statement gives us criteria for evaluating how well we are doing what we are here to do.

After the introduction in which the facilitator explained the process of creating and purpose of having a parish mission statement, the listening session continued. The larger group broke into smaller groups, with each group discussing one question similar to one of the following:

• What is our parish story? How did we come to be a parish community?

• What would Jesus say we should be doing in our parish today?

• What makes this parish different from other parishes?

• Who will we serve as a parish?

Each small group then shared the specifics of its respective discussion on a newsprint, an overhead transparency, or by some other visual means. A general discussion followed so that people could speak to topics that were not discussed in their own small group. These additional ideas were recorded as well.

St. Martin's held several such listening sessions, some in the daytime, some in the evening. Over time, a good deal of curiosity and energy were generated, along with insights and direction for the writing group to fashion an initial draft of the parish mission statement.

Drafting a Mission Statement and Presenting It to the Parish

St. Martin's final mission statement was brief. It contained a few sentences that named and described the parish, and connected it with the larger Church and the mission of Jesus Christ. Gleaning the wisdom and insights offered by parishioners during listening sessions, the writing group captured the "why" of St. Martin's existence and in a few more sentences that gave the general direction in which it needed to move as a Catholic community.

After the document was reworked, a Sunday was selected for presenting it to the parishioners for ratification. At each liturgy, the pastor spoke about mission in general, and this St. Martin's mission statement at each liturgy in particular. Then, when the document was formally presented by the pastoral council, enthusiastic applause erupted. Each parishioner was given a card containing the mission statement. A mission statement plaque, which was part of the presentation as well, now hangs in the church, and each Sunday's bulletin carries the mission statement in its entirety.

Integrating the Mission Statement Into Various Ministries

Crafting and publicizing the mission statement was just the beginning. Every parish staff person and every committee leader was asked for ideas about how to use the mission statement in some way. In parish meetings, people reminded one another in explicit ways how this group's reason for existence and its specific activities were connected to carrying out the mission. The parish council was determined that the mission statement would not become a lost paper in a file, but would be a living statement of identity and action.

Here are some questions that may be valuable in crafting your parish's mission statement.

- What could be done to make your parish more effective in Word, Worship, Service, and Community?

- What could be the value of revisiting or creating your own parish mission statement? Who would be involved in studying/discussing this issue?

- What would you do differently compared to how St. Martin's pastoral council developed its parish mission statement?

- What do you think they did well/effectively? Why?

- What are the next steps that you think should be taken after crafting an acceptable parish mission statement?

From Mission to Plan

The next stage for St. Martin's parish council, now that this basic groundwork had been completed, was to begin a planning process as an outgrowth of the mission statement.

Individuals who go through life on automatic pilot rarely, if ever, live up to their full potential. Rather, they experience life in a passive, unenergetic, and meaningless manner. The same is true for committees, programs, projects, and even parishes. The closer we are to the dream or vision of what we can be, the more we can use the gifts and talents God has given us to use for the good of others.

The early Christians stayed close to the vision: "What you do to the least of these...." What vision are we following in our parish? What does the vision call us to be and to do? St. Martin's leaders considered these kinds of questions as they focused on carrying out the mission statement they had created. In this framework, the planning process began.

The pastor led the council in clarifying why the council members were undertaking pastoral planning in the first place. Pastoral planning envisions what the parish could and should be doing. It evaluates the needs of the community and it then sets goals for the parish in light of its mission. Pastoral planning translates goals into objectives and to the time lines needed to implement these objectives. And all of this is done using listening and discernment, prayer and reflection. Finally, pastoral planning puts in place a method for evaluating, over time, what has been planned and accomplished.

Listening Again

So, the planners begin again. Once more, the St. Martin's parish leadership turned to the community and listened to what it had to say, using a combination of questionnaires and group assemblies to hear the hopes and dreams of the people. And, in listening to the hopes and dreams of the people, they could hear the needs of the community.

A subcommittee gathered pertinent data, such as local demographics, parish statistics, trends of financial support within the parish, and any other helpful information. Questionnaires were also used to gather information. They were mailed to parish households, and they were asked to pray over it, complete it, and return it to the parish after answering the questions. The questionnaire led people to describe their hopes and dreams or to paint word pictures of how the parish might look if it was to follow its mission over the coming years. The questionnaire followed the same divisions as the mission statement reflection process: Word, Worship, Service, and Community. The parish mission statement served as the heart of each of these areas.

The second-tier listening sessions follow the same pattern as before. Rooted in prayer, the groups dreamed together. Small-group discussions were centered around the same four divisions as the questionnaire. This format kept the discussions focused on the future rather than becoming a forum for complaining or for dealing with other issues on complaints, problem solving, or other parish issues. Later, they heard from each small group and wove their dreams together. People became energized by these dreams and hopes. The process helped underline the importance of the mission statement as central to everything planned.

The pastor and council were pleased with the participation of so many parishioners and the expression of many ideas; now they had the task of translating hopes into concrete plans. This phase of the process involved setting goals and objectives.

Goals and Objectives

Goals are *general* statements of an outcome, or a *general* result to be accomplished. Goals, brief and clearly stated, tell what the results of each effort will look like, and are usually accomplished in three to five years. The St. Martin's planning group decided to organize these five-year goals according to the categories the planning process had been using thus far: Word, Worship, Service, and Community. The planning team looked closely at the data—which reflected the voice of the people—to determine these priorities. In some cases, the goal called for something new to be created. More often, however, it stated what kind of improvement or strengthening was needed in an existing area. They did not address specifics, nor did the goals name *how* something was to be accomplished. That was the task of translating the goals into *objectives*.

An objective is the *exact* statement of who will do what by when. Thus, St. Martin's parish council was now ready to take the next step: creating a time line for when and how the goals would be carried out for each of the five years. Now the planning process became very concrete and practical. Each objective would be delineated by who would do what by when.

The parish council knew that, in most cases, objectives could be written with the greatest clarity and brevity by the staff person or parish ministry commission charged with a given area. In such cases, the objectives were approved by the supervisor or the council liaison representing that particular area. In other cases, the council committee itself specified the objectives. All objectives were carefully written so as to be realistic, but still challenging. Each one was also quite specific with regard to who would benefit by the completion of this objective, as well as being specific about what would be done and by when.

The parish council realized how important it was for the St. Martin's parish leadership to both empower and motivate staff and parishioners who would be responsible for carrying out each objective. This was the only way the goals would be reached.

Implementation is where the rubber meets the road—and St. Martin's council knew that engaging the right people to implement the objectives was critical. They were also very clear that carrying out the objectives themselves was not their role. Rather, their job was to plan, empower, and oversee. They could serve as resources, but it would take the gifts and talents of many parishioners within the community—existing committees and organizations as well as newly created groups—to bring the parish vision to reality.

How Are We Doing?

All endeavors need a process by which success and failure can be assessed and evaluated. *Assessment* means taking a regular look at how things are going, and thus it calls for setting up a regular system that indicates how the plan is working. While it is clearly not the job of the parish council to manage the day-to-day operational implementation of the parish plan, it is responsible for instituting a general tracking system to monitor how the plan is working. And, at the end of the year, when the parish council takes a new look at each objective, it will know what, if any, adjustments need to be made. What's working and why? Is there room for yet further improvement? What's not working and why not? What should be done about it?

Assessment and evaluation are also critical to the next planning process, for plans always need to be refreshed and refocused. Assessment and evaluation tells where to begin in painting the picture of where the parish is, in seeing and analyzing problems with past goals and objectives, and in naming what needs to be celebrated as success and accomplishment. Assessment is not just for the purpose of critique, but is an important part of expressing gratitude for a mission accomplished.

The first anniversary party at St. Martin's brought together many people who cared about the parish and who had shared their time and talents in the implementation process. They ate and drank and prayed and listened to the progress reports, and congratulated one another on their contributions to making the parish mission statement a lived reality in the life of the parish and the neighborhood. It was a celebration not to be missed!

Here are some additional questions that may be helpful in looking at the evaluation component of the parish plan.

• What am I thankful for in our parish?

• What would help our parish be more mission effective?

• What will I do to be part of bringing that about?

Resources for Additional Reading

Deegan, Arthur X., II, ed. *Developing a Vibrant Parish Pastoral Council.* Mahwah, N.J.: Paulist Press, 1995.

Gilder, Constance. *The Ministry of Pastoral Planning.* Archdiocese of Baltimore: Division of Planning and Council Services.

Gubish, Mary Ann and Susan Jenny, S.C., with Arlene McGannon. *Revisioning the Parish Pastoral Council.* Mahwah, N.J.: Paulist Press, 2001.

McKinney, Mary Benet. *Sharing Wisdom: A Process for Group Decision Making.* Chicago, IL: Thomas More Publishing, 1998.

Sofield, Loughlan and Donald Kuhn. *The Collaborative Leader: Listening to the Wisdom of God's People.* Notre Dame, IN: Ave Maria Press, 1995.

CHAPTER 4

Community Building: Christian Community As Heart of the Parish

~

Where two or three are gathered in my name, I am there among them.

MATTHEW 18:20

From the beginning of our Church to the anticipated eternity in heaven, we are presented with the ideal of community, the model of Christian living. Jesus, his apostles and disciples, formed the original Church community. They spent time together; they knew each other well. They talked, shared meals, prayed together, and, yes, even argued together. In the sharing of their joys and sorrows, their grieving and their healing, they were deeply connected with one another's lives. They shared their stories, their joys and sorrows. They mourned together when Lazarus died, they brought Jesus to their sick family members such as Peter's mother-in-law, they chatted together as they walked.

Compared with what we know about Jesus, his apostles and disciples, we know very little about heaven. We do know, however, that heaven will be a sharing in the community experience of the Trinity, which is the model of a perfect community. So community is central at the beginning of our Christian story and also at its end.

The Scriptures also tell us that community was at the heart of the early believers' way of life. We read: "They devoted themselves to the apostles' instruction and the communal life, to the breaking of the bread

and to prayers…Those who believed shared all things in common…
dividing everything on the basis of each one's needs" (Acts 2:42–45). While
this kind of intimate community—one of total commitment and total
sharing—is far from what most parishes experience, more and more
people hunger and strive for some kind of experience of community.
Likewise, pastoral leaders give increasing attention to how to create a
community within the parish structure, although *create* is too strong a
word perhaps because community cannot be forced or mandated. There
are, of course, ways to help develop and support community life, to facilitate its growth and health, and many parish staffs put great energy
into those things that enable and encourage just that.

And we need it. When an elderly woman named Pearl was asked what
happiness is, she answered without hesitation, "Happiness is *belonging*."
When James O'Halloran describes this encounter in *Signs of Hope*, he
then goes on to say, "Happiness is belonging to a family where I am loved
and accepted as I am. Happiness is belonging to a community where I
am loved and accepted as I am."

Every human being hungers to some degree for connectedness, for
belonging. Even the most introverted people have the human need to
belong; to have their life, their experience, matter to others; to be understood and to share with others. In our deepest selves, we long for a har-
mony that is not available in the larger world. We hope to find a safer
place than the world, a place where our sadness and our struggles might
be lifted up within the hope of others. We want a place where we are
known—and accepted anyway.

Yet, society today seems obsessed with individualism and personal
rights. Furthermore, modern life often rushes people from one activity
to the next, with no time to really connect with others and without occasions for developing close relationships. Families often live at great dis-
tances from each other, in different parts of the country, sometimes on
different continents. In the midst of this, people suffer a deep and driving hunger for connectedness, for community.

The rise of mega-churches for mainstream and evangelical Protes-
tant denominations is just a step ahead of the Catholic Church in this
country, as the clergy shortage has put dioceses either in the midst or on
the brink of merging and closing parishes. In place after place, this means
expanding existing buildings or constructing larger ones to accommo-
date more people to attend the fewer liturgies that can be celebrated.

Although the development of small communities within our parishes predates the shortage of priests, it nonetheless underlines the urgency of searching for ways to connect people within a large congregation.

On the whole, we Catholics have not been good at developing a sense of authentic community. The late Bishop John J. Sullivan often told the story of a man getting out of his car for Sunday Mass in the pouring rain, and another man running over and sharing his umbrella until they both were inside. Turning to express his appreciation, the first man said, "I've been going to this church for several years and this is the first time anyone has even spoken to me." Chagrined, the other man responded, "I just came here this morning with my wife who is Catholic. I belong to the Lutheran church down the street." We can do better—and we often do. But it takes commitment to cultivate community in our parishes.

How to Do It

When the leadership of the parish speaks often about the need to grow as a community, that growth is more likely to happen. Discussing and brainstorming about what can be done to enrich life as a community helps all groups and individuals take responsibility for making it happen. This challenge can be given to every group, every organization, every individual, in the parish—and given often. When community building is an explicit goal, people become responsible for making—or at least helping—it happen.

The primary means of creating a sense of community within the parish is the primary reason we gather as a community—the Sunday liturgy. Good liturgy creates community. When our weekly liturgical celebration is indeed a celebration, when it engages people in praying together and experiencing good ritual, it bonds them one with another. Successful liturgical experiences require that care and attention be paid to preparing for these celebrations, for rich liturgy doesn't happen automatically, without consciously, conscientiously, and regularly working toward it. Priests, parish staff, and liturgy committees who take time to study, plan, and reflect on the liturgy all help make it not only a more meaningful liturgy but one that is community-planned and focused as well.

Good liturgy includes three key components:

- *Preaching* that is Scripture-based and connects with life during the week is critical. The homily should both comfort and challenge, and play a significant role in liturgy. The Eucharist, is "the source and summit" of our community life, and not an experience in private prayer.

- *Music* that is beautiful, singable, well-done, and appropriate to the liturgical season and to the part of the Mass in which it is included makes an enormous difference in how we pray as a community.

- *Involvement of parishioners* in both the preparation and roles within the liturgy connects them more intimately and is a powerful sign that it is indeed a community prayer.

With these components in mind, consider the following community-building experiences:

Sacramental Celebrations

Celebrating the sacraments within the community is a community-building experience as well as being good theology. If the community is not accustomed to infant baptism during Sunday liturgy, for example, it may take some getting used to, but it is worth the time and effort. When the community renews its baptismal promises together, when it commits to supporting the parents in raising the child, when it laughs together at the infant's antics and applauds in welcome, when it has the opportunity to meet the family over coffee afterwards, connections and community spirit result.

Sending Rituals

More and more parishes conduct a brief "sending ritual" for those going out in the name of the community, such as taking Communion to the sick, delivering food to the hungry, or visiting those in prisons. A brief blessing offered over these people at Mass reminds the community what is being done in its name, and offers an insight into the persons undertaking the ministry. The man you've seen at Mass, the woman you've greeted at the market now stand before you and are connected to you in a deeper way.

Community Reconciliation Celebrations

Parishes find that community celebrations of the sacrament of reconciliation enhance parishioners' experience of this sacrament and bring friends and strangers together in something serious and, if well done, beautiful. Reflective music, an atmosphere of candles and quiet, enough priests to help avoid long delays, and a brief homily take little planning compared to the rich rewards of the community experience. Many dioceses rotate these services within a deanery during Advent and Lent, so that the priests are able to join one another in a different service each week so there are a sufficient number of confessors.

Praying for One Another

Praying for one another creates another community bond. Listing in the bulletin the names of those in the parish who are sick, or praying for them at daily Mass (praying especially for anyone having surgery) if they so wish to have it done, is a strong way to build community. Some parishes have a "prayer wall" in the vestibule of the church, where people can write intentions for which they wish people to pray. Many places have a "phone tree," which involves a chain of communication that informs the entire parish of urgent prayer needs. Parish "pray-ers" often are the housebound or those who can't physically be involved in the community in other ways but are glad to pray for the community's needs.

Special Services for the Feasts of All Saints and All Souls

Another meaningful community prayer experience is an annual service during November for anyone whose loved one has died during the year. The parish Book of the Dead is read, and Scripture and music provide the heart of the service.

Hospitality

Some parishes begin simply by offering coffee and donuts after Mass to encourage people to stay and get acquainted, challenging them to meet someone new rather than visiting with old friends or acquaintances. Inviting new parishioners or visitors to stand and be welcomed at the beginning of the Mass helps regular community members recognize newcomers later, at coffee and donuts. These informal gestures are first steps in helping people connect.

RCIA Blessings

When new members journey through the process of the Rite of Christian Initiation of Adults (RCIA) with the community, they not only become acquainted and bonded with it, but community members can grow closer together. It should always be a function of the community to walk with them—whether as team members, sponsors, support workers, or "pray-ers and blessers" of the catechumens and candidates.

Family-Centered Catechetical Programs

Such programs help people connect and share what is important. Family-centered catechisis need not be a large parishwide campaign. Gatherings that include even a few families who meet regularly in their homes to share their faith with each other and with their children will enhance the sense of community throughout the parish. Sharing meals together, engaging in service projects as a group, utilizing catechetical materials, and talking freely about the place of their faith in daily life enrich individual lives, family life, and the life of the parish community. Since the 1970s, there has been a steady movement of parishes that offer this option for such intergenerational faith formation.

Laity Training

Community is developed when parishioners take leadership roles in educational endeavors for one another. People connect when they experience one another as leaders of prayer, facilitators of small prayer or study groups, leaders in faith-formation classes, and so on. It is the responsibility of the parish to prepare such laity through education, materials, and other resources. Training for groups such as Stephen Ministry provides ongoing service to the homebound and those who are ill, while helping to keep them connected to the community. Bringing the needs of these people back into the community for prayer connects all involved.

Parish Newsletters

Monthly parish newsletters, usually compiled by volunteers, are especially effective when they include photographs of past parish activities and news items about upcoming events.

Care Packages

A parish on the East Coast gathers parents and friends of college students, along with anyone else interested, and sends "care packages" at exam time to the community members away at school. These packages include food, cartoons, tension-breaking toys such as frisbees, and cards and notes that have been posted for weeks on the church bulletin board collecting signatures. A sense of community deepens among those gathered to assemble these care packages, and the sense of community outreach to college students increases the likelihood that the students will return to the parish during vacation times.

"Needs Groups"

One pastor said there was more community happening in the church basement than in the worship space upstairs. He appreciated the value of allowing and even encouraging "needs groups" to use the church facilities for meetings—groups such as Alcoholics Anonymous, quilting groups, tai chi for seniors, basketball for teens, baby-sitting for young parents during volleyball, and any other groups that needed a secure environment for their gatherings. When these people come to worship together on Sunday, they have a different relationship with one another and with God, because of what happened downstairs on Wednesday night.

Parish Directories

Many parishes have pictorial directories of parishioners. Some directories include lists of all organizations and activities and the contact person for each, encouraging people to feel free to phone any of them.

Parish Calendars

A small town in central Illinois gives its parish calendar a high profile. It covers the entire wall of the church vestibule and is included on the back of the bulletin each week. Every activity and a contact person for each event is clearly noted on the calendar. Parishioners have no excuse for not knowing what is happening.

Because Christians are people of hope, we believe that with God's help we can overcome our human weaknesses and differences, and experience the fullness of community. Like marriage, community is good—and it requires effort. One of the fruits of this effort of building community in our parishes is a focus on good spirituality. When a parish puts energy into creating community, a good spirituality emerges that enriches the larger body of the church while helping people both within and outside the parish.

In *Parish in the Next Millennium,* William Bausch cites fundamentalism as a threat to community. Given the negative trends in the world today, such as political assassinations, family deterioration, and crime, the fundamentalists feel one can no longer trust time but can trust only in eternity. This, Bausch explains, is why they teach "timeless truth, absolute commandments, and literal Bible passages, and wage war against left-wing destroyers of faith, family, and national security."

Fundamentalism is flourishing among Catholics, Jewish Zionists, Islamic, Hindu, Marxist, and Hindu groups in reaction to the modern world's dangers. Among Catholics, Father Bausch explains, there are fundamentalists on both sides, conservatives and liberals. Conservative fundamentalists want to return to such things as a strict interpretation of infallibility, a pyramid structure of order, firm authority, religious visions, and so on, while on the other side, liberals want a form of plurality and democracy as appeared in the first decades of Christianity. He calls the polarization between the two groups a scandal that is sapping the energy of the Church. Certainly it is a serious obstacle to Christian community.

Let Us Break Bread Together

"Breaking bread together" is one of the most powerful ways to build community. Food and fellowship following church events can be as simple as coffee and donuts a few times a year on Welcome Sunday, when new parishioners are recognized. It can be as elaborate as champagne and finger food after the Easter Vigil in celebration of the newly baptized and confirmed. Many parishes have an annual picnic that is as simple as a "bring-your-own-food" affair, and includes clowns, games, and live music. These are all ways of developing the familiarity and the relational glue that enhance community identity.

Monthly dinners in homes are easily organized to provide opportunities for diverse groups to break bread together. One parish model is the Dinner for Eight, a once-a-month potluck for anyone who chooses to participate. Groups rotate homes with the host or hostess providing the entree, and each person attending bringing another part of the meal. New parishioners are encouraged to attend a few times to meet a variety of people. Some parishioners attend a few times a year, others regularly. There is no agenda other than enjoying one another's company.

Chapter five briefly deals with the progressive stages of a community that begins politely and moves through dealing with inevitable conflict. A maturing process is necessary and requires acknowledging the realities that beset a community in stages of growth. In a sense, we wish for heaven here on earth all the while knowing that this ideal is not possible. We don't want arguments and disagreements within a our community. In lukewarm communities, people stay connected, sort of, but not in any depth of investment. Rather, they are polite and only superficially connected. And even in the "best" communities, where there is conscious desire and movement to build community, we are someplace between the story of Bishop Sullivan and the Garden of Eden before the Fall.

But because we are people of hope, we must press on, in spite of our failures in developing a community experience, or in spite of it not being the perfect experience we imagined. We continue, knowing that we are doing what we can, to bring about the kingdom here on earth, doing what we can to meet real human needs for connectedness, doing what we can to live the gospel mandates. For what binds our church communities together is not simply friendship and personal need, but shared faith and commitment to Jesus' dreams—both about the present and the future coming of the reign of God. It is our shared values, our ideas, and our common purpose that make parish communities, communities of believers, a unique and life-giving experience.

Here are some questions that will help you explore the current status of your own parish community:

- When have you felt most connected with a community? What was it that provided that experience?

- Why is the connection with other people central to the celebration of the Eucharist, making it a community prayer not a private prayer?

- How can you contribute to community connections in your parish?

- What can your parish council, committees, and organizations do to foster community?

Resources for Additional Reading

Bausch, William J. *The Hands-On Parish: Reflections and Suggestions for Fostering Community.* Mystic, CT: Twenty-Third Publications, 1991.

Bausch, William J. *The Total Parish Manual: Everything You Need to Empower Your Faith Community.* Mystic, CT: Twenty-Third Publications, 1996.

Lee, Bernard J., S.M. *The Catholic Experience of Small Christian Communities.* Mahwah, N.J.: Paulist Press, 2000.

O'Halloran, James. *Signs of Hope*, Maryknoll, NY: Orbis Books, 1991.

CHAPTER 5

Enabling Small Groups: Connecting Individuals

~

Because of their special vocation, the laity seek the kingdom of God by engaging in temporal affairs and ordering them according to the plan of God. They work for the sanctification of the world from within by fulfilling their own particular duties.

"DOGMATIC CONSTITUTION ON THE CHURCH,"

PARAGRAPH 31

The intentional community comes together to enjoy a degree of communality that a larger community seldom attains or enjoys. An intentional community, presumably, comes together to share life with one another, to grow in a depth of faith, hope, and love and to be united in their service of the larger community.

JOHN HAUGHEY, S.J.

Community is the primary context in which people grow in their understanding and awareness of God's revelation. This was true for the communities from which the gospels came, and it is true for us today. We begin our faith journey usually in the family community, the domestic church. For adults in the Catholic Church today, faith formation is happening more and more within small communities in parishes. As people bring their life experience, their concrete daily life, to the community, the group brings additional experience to bear on it, to clarify its meaning and connection with faith. In that reflection process, faith is deepened, knowledge increases, and insight happens—and thus our faith, knowledge, and insight about our role as Christians in the world grow. This growth in intimacy with others and with the Spirit gives us the courage to live our lives as Christ has taught.

Michael Cowan describes a small community as being both like and unlike a family and a task group. It is like a family in that it strives for a sense of trust, a feeling of belonging and close sharing. It is unlike a family in that it dare not become self-focused or absorbed in *only* the fellowship and support side of the experience. It is like a task-centered group in that by being gospel-centered participants must look outside of themselves and the group and be led to action as a result of bonding and community experience. It is unlike a task group in that its goals are not merely external, but also internally focused.

Sociologists have long taught that any community focused only on itself is doomed to failure. The other side of that coin is that a group engaged *only* in action inevitably experiences burnout and discouragement, because it is not grounded in support and sharing, and thus is without deep roots in the reason for action—faith. In fact, both of these components—tending to relationships and gospel sharing within the group, and lived action outside the group—are necessary and interdependent. Neither can exist alone if the experience of group membership is to be rich, fulfilling, and Christian.

Taking Time

Many people today live a high-speed, fast-forward lifestyle that does not allow time and place for reflection. In fact, as a rule, modern life aggressively militates against reflection. Yet, noticing what happens to us day to day and learning from that life experience is essential to human and Christian life. The small community can fill this void by providing a structure of time and place. It brings together a group that is willing to join together to reflect regularly on its life experience. This group reflection is a valuable way to grow and continue to appreciate the sacredness of daily life. Such a community is a true gift.

In a real sense, the small community is countercultural in our individualistic times—having the time and space for regular reflection is itself countercultural. And any such attempt to be countercultural is effective to the extent that we do it, not alone, but with others.

Over a period of time, members of a small community learn the habit of asking how God might be speaking to them in their ordinary daily events. They eventually develop new lenses to see their life as holy, because they discover Christ there at home, in the workplace, in social encounters. Over time, they challenge themselves to act on the gospel values they have committed themselves to live. This, too, is easier to do within a group. Maybe it's saying out loud to the group what I intend or want to do that gives me the impetus to take action. Maybe it's a group action that I can join for courage and effectiveness. Maybe it's taking an idea, that was incubated in the small group, out into the larger parish community for broader support and ownership.

A Popular Phenomenon

A Lilly Endowment study titled *The Catholic Experience of Small Christian Communities* (Paulist Press, 2000) shows that there is an estimated 45,000 to 50,000 of these small communities throughout the United States alone. These groups meet weekly, biweekly, or monthly to engage in faith sharing, Scripture reading, discussion, and prayer. The study shows that family and prayer are issues of overwhelming importance to these group members. Amazingly, their weekly participation in the Eucharist is 93 percent, as compared with 32 percent of the general Catholic population. It is the desire to learn about God and the need for the support of others that motivates members to belong to such groups—and what keeps them involved in the community is the quality of the relationships that develop over time.

Inevitably, as faith is lived more consciously and actively by individuals in small groups, the life of the parish is enriched. Typically, for example, parish-based small church communities are eager for a strong, active relationship with their pastors. They are not interested in rescuing the parish or the Church, but rather in living out their baptism more fully, and in serving and evangelizing others through witness to a Christian life.

What the Groups Are Not

Mary Louise was delighted when her parish provided the opportunity for small groups to gather during the lenten season. She was equally pleased when, after Easter, her group decided to continue meeting on a weekly basis. Although the group was quite diverse, its community prayer and reflection was rich and supportive of Mary Louise's desire to learn and grow in her faith.

After a year or so of meeting every week, however, tragedy struck one of the group members: Lee Ann's young child was killed in a car accident. Through this dark and painful time, the entire group supported Lee Ann in many ways, both as individuals and as a community. They were with her during the first devastating weeks. Gradually, as time went on, Lee Ann began to talk about nothing else when the community met. For a long time, people understood this, of course, and continued to be present and patient with her. But after several months, Mary Louise began to feel uncomfortable. The group was no longer focused on its original mission but had, in effect, become Lee Ann's grief support group. Although Mary Louise gently suggested to Lee Ann that she join the parish group for those recovering from loss, nothing changed. Mary Louise eventually dropped out of the group because her own needs were not being met and she felt that confronting Lee Ann would seem cruel and un-Christian.

Small communities such as this are not support groups for dealing with crises such as illness or death; there are other important transitory groups designed solely for this purpose. Nor are they support groups for dealing with addictions. While such groups provide a priceless contribution to the healing and recovery of people in need, they are different in form and focus. For example, although addiction-recovery groups are sometimes Christian or God-centered in various ways, the faith dimension is not essential to the group members' interaction. Rather, they focus on a problem, with most of the group's energy being directed inward. Unfortunately, Mary Louise's experience indicates a lack of leadership training to handle such situations.

Theological Reflection in a Small Group

Small faith communities are committed to the gospel and to making the reign of the gospel and Christ's example more alive and operative in the broader community and in the world. They do this by more consciously and deliberately living their own faith. This is accomplished primarily through theological reflection.

The basic premise of such theological reflection is that there is truly an intimate relationship between our lives and our religious heritage, our beliefs. Theological reflection is the process that helps us discover that relationship, to see what one of them says to the other. To the extent that we see and try to live out that connection, to make our faith relevant and vibrant in all parts of our lives, we are able to live an authentic Christian life.

Sometimes people are put off by the term *theological reflection,* because it sounds like something academic or abstract. The process, however, is actually quite simple and easy to engage in. In fact, people often do theological reflection unconsciously. Here, in the small community, it is done consciously and not alone, but with the experience of other believers joined together.

Theological reflection is, first of all, just that—*reflection.* It is the effort to look at our life experience—whether it's our experience as an individual, a community, a family, a church—and examine that experience in relation to our religious tradition, our faith. In the process of theological reflection, we ask certain questions: What does Scripture and the wisdom of the ages say to my daily life experience? How do they challenge it? Clarify it? Affirm it? And, what will I do as a result of this insight? This conversation between experience and faith is made all the richer when it is done in the experience of a reflective, prayerful, faith-filled group.

Parish-Centered Communities

In some places, the entire parish is completely organized into small groups. Other parishes offer voluntary groups that involve only those parishioners who wish to belong. Some parishes begin with an organized process or program such as that available from RENEW International which trains leaders and provides materials. Others use seasonal helps or topical small-group guides from religious publishers or organizations. In some places, small communities spring up on their own and have broader purposes and different ways of being organized and facilitated.

But what do the small groups *do*? How is a small-group session structured? This, too, varies from place to place. Most parish-initiated groups are Scripture-based prayer groups that form community, reflect and pray, and eventually lead to some kind of voluntary action. Everyone in the group spends time in prayer: silent, formal, ritual-based, or spontaneous. Many ongoing groups use the Scriptures for the liturgical season as their starting point.

Many small groups follow a process similar to what RENEW International outlines:

- Coming together: People gather in the home of one of the group's members, and informal visiting takes place as people "catch up" with one another. The sharing of lives, whether getting to know each other in initial stages of the group or hearing about what's transpired with a particular situation or problem since the last conversation, is an important part of the group growing together. Connecting with the lives of others enables members to share more deeply and more comfortably, and to share about the real life issues with which they are dealing every day. This coming together adds to the richness of the life of the group.

- Prayer: The leader then invites everyone to gather and collect themselves for prayer, which might be a brief period of silence, a song, a spontaneous prayer, or a formal prayer read aloud.

- The gospel: The gospel for the week is then proclaimed, followed by a quiet time during which people reflect on what seems to emerge for them from the gospel reading. This reflection might be based on a phrase, a word, or perhaps an idea that came from each person's hearing of God's Word. Group members are encouraged to mention these reflective comments aloud if they wish.

• Reflection and discussion: Following the Scripture reading, the prepared reflection is read aloud and questions to stimulate conversation are discussed by the group. Because this is not the same as Scripture study, but rather is prayer leading to a deepening of faith and a desire to act on that faith, the discussion is very directly connected to life. This is a time of talking and listening, and of learning from one another's insights and experience—all of which is the heartbeat of a small community. Here is where the relationship between faith and life is seriously probed. Here also is where people gain insight and encouragement from one another. During these discussions, the group leader does not perform the role of expert nor that of teacher, but rather serves as the facilitator who helps keep things on track and encourages participation by everyone present. People are expected to share at their own comfort level, but everyone is equally responsible for contributing to the conversation in some way. A basic and inviolate understanding among group members is that confidences shared are kept within the group.

Because living faith leads to action, small-faith communities share ideas about how to put their insights into action in their daily lives. Thus, discussions eventually bring certain questions to the forefront: What will I do? How can I carry these beliefs and convictions into my home, my workplace, my parish or civic communities? What might we do as a group as a result of our prayers, reflections, and insights?

• Ending prayer: Although the entire process is truly prayer, an ending prayer formally closes the session. Again, this varies from formal prayer to prepared prayer to spontaneous prayer to a ritual action. Whatever form the prayer takes, it is in some way a *Collect*, that is, it collects what the group has discovered and decided, and offers it to God, asking for the needed help to live out this renewed faith.

• What happens next? Because we are creatures of habit living busy lives, accountability is a helpful motivator. Thus, many groups find it helpful to begin their next session with each person describing how they did with the resolution they made during the previous gathering. This review provides encouragement, affirmation, and sometimes problem solving by the whole group.

Two important questions involve the length of a small-group session and its size. The length of any small-group meeting depends on the purpose of the group and whether the gathering is connected to other events and activities, such as a meal or a meeting. It is, however, very important that the group negotiate the length of time, and that this time frame be diligently respected each time the group gathers. It is also critical that when people "sign up" they are clear about how many sessions will be involved. Are they making a commitment for the six weeks of Lent? Or is their commitment an ongoing one? Or is it for a certain number of sessions with an option to renegotiate? It is this sort of clarity that fosters commitment.

Finding the right size group also is important. If the group is too small, it lacks the richness it needs and the ability to sustain itself when there are absences. If the group is too large, some people will feel there's not enough opportunity for everyone to join unless the meeting goes on for a long time. Eight to ten people seems to be a good size to offset these kinds of problems.

The irony of a small group is that it is at once a sanctuary or haven where people can speak freely about what is most important in life, but it is also the place where members are challenged to change and grow, where *status quo* in living the faith is not allowed to be comfortable. These two opposites are precisely why small groups can be the rich home that thousands and thousands of people join and cherish.

How Are We Doing?

Experience teaches that developing a community is a long-term process. Patience is needed to allow time for people to get to know one another and to ease into the rhythm of the process. Relationships, trust, and confidence with and in the group require time to develop. Experts explain that groups go through predictable stages of development. The following material is adapted from Charles J. Keating, *The Leadership Book*, Mahwah, N.J.: Paulist Press, 1995.

At the beginning, there is the Polite-With-Each-Other Stage, during which people hide their own insecurities and work to be accepted and liked by the group. During this stage, conversation is usually superficial. Gradually, however, people let down their guard and become themselves, relying less on the group leader to enrich the dialogue.

Next comes the Questioning-Our-Purpose Stage. During this time, members check out whether they belong, question the purpose of the group's existence, discover boundaries, and establish ground rules. Group members gradually internalize the agreed upon purpose, and are more at ease with one another.

The Bid-For-Power Stage comes next. During this time, individuals seek to influence and eventually decide the leadership in the group. During this stage, conflict needs to be faced openly and clearly lest it go "underground" and keep the group from moving ahead.

Moving forward, the group now comes to the Constructive Stage, when members are ready to truly listen and hear one another, sharing at a deeper level and feeling they can trust others to accept them. By this time, the group enjoys a clear sense of identity, which means that if new members join, they will have to go through the previous stages in order to reach where the others are and realize a sense of comfort, trust, and purpose.

Finally, there is the Esprit Stage, where a strong loyalty and even dependence exists. Here the group's challenge is to face problems and conflicts squarely and not give in to the temptation to avoid them lest the good feelings disappear. In fact, the opposite is true. Failing to face problems and conflicts risks the group's reversion to an earlier stage of development.

How Is It Going?

There are certain signs that will indicate if the group is functioning as it should and accomplishing what it intends. Some of these signs are identifiable according to the stages of development outlined above. But what about its central purpose? The following questions can help the group discern whether it is truly helping the community members in their quest for a richer Christian life:

- Are members experiencing more clarity about God's presence in their daily lives? Are they able to live, more deliberately and clearly, with an awareness of God's presence?

- Are members growing in an understanding of their faith, especially what the gospels teach us as the way to go about being a Christian?

- Are group members more committed to action, and does that include action outside the community as well as within it?

- Has the experience of community grown richer and more trustworthy over time?

- Has the spiritual or interior life of the group's members deepened as a result of this time together?

Small Christian communities are the result of effective leadership, shared responsibility, and pastoral planning. They can be the backbone of a strong community identity and the vehicle for continuous faith formation within the parish. It takes planning and work to get small Christian communities started, however, and it takes much sustained nurturing to support them—but the fruits of these groups within a parish are evident in a short period of time and are more than worth the effort.

Resources for Additional Reading

Currier, Richard, and Frances Gram. *Forming a Small Christian Community: A Personal Journey.* Mystic, CT: Twenty-Third Publications, 1992.

Foley, Gerald, and Timothy Schmaltz. *Connecting Faith and Life: Holiness of Ordinary Life.* Kansas City, MO: Sheed & Ward, 1987.

Golas, Suzanne, C.S.J.P. *Called to Lead: Leadership Development in a Small Community Context, Group Development & Leader's Manual.* Mahwah, N.J.: Paulist Press, 1994.

Kleissler, Thomas A., Margo A. LeBert, and Mary C. McGuinness. *Small Christian Communities: A Vision of Hope.* Mahwah, N.J.: Paulist Press, 1991.

Moriarty, Robert K. "Parish and Small Church Communities," *America,* May 7, 2001.

O'Halloran, James. *Signs of Hope: Developing Small Christian Communities*. Maryknoll, N.Y.: Orbis Books, 1991.

"Small Christian Communities." *The Catholic World*. Mahwah, N.J.: Paulist Press, July/August 1991.

"Small Groups: Micro and Macro Church." *Chicago Studies*. Mundelein, IL: Civitas Dei Foundation, August 1992.

Whitehead, James D. and Evelyn Eaton Whitehead. *Community of Faith: Models and Strategies for Developing Christian Communities*. San Francisco: HarperSanFrancisco, 1984.

CHAPTER 6

Parish Pastoral Council:
A Leadership Community

~

The parish exists not for itself, but for the mission of Christ. And so people are called forth to minister to one another in the parish community, as well as to those around them where they live.

THE PARISH: A PEOPLE, A MISSION, A STRUCTURE.
NATIONAL CONFERENCE OF CATHOLIC BISHOPS, 1980

O ne might ask why do we need a parish at all. As the above quote explains, parishes exist to help lead the parish to become what it is meant to be, to fulfill the mission of Christ.

Some people may think the parish exists for them, because they need it. Others may view the parish as a kind of spiritual gas station where they go to get a fill-up once a week. Some people may see it as a place for contact with others like themselves, or as the sponsor of schools that provide an education for their children. Others may see it as the closest thing to the community that the disciples of Jesus experienced.

While there may be pieces of the reality in each of these notions, the parish, in fact, exists not for itself but to continue the mission of Christ. The *only* reason the Church exists is simply to continue the mission work of Jesus. And our diocese and our parish exist to carry out that work in our corner of the world, at this particular moment in history.

The Mission

How does the parish carry out the mission of the Church? The parish carries out this mission in several ways.

- The parish carries out the mission of the Church, of which Christ is head, by proclaiming the Word of God.

- The parish carries out the mission of the Church through worship and the sacraments.

- The parish carries out the mission of the Church through service to others.

- The parish carries out the mission of the Church through gathering as a community.

Proclaiming the Word

Jesus Christ proclaimed the Word throughout his public life and ministry. In the Church today, the Word is proclaimed in several ways. The Church literally proclaims the Word in the Eucharist and in other worship services. Listening to the Scriptures and hearing them broken open in homilies instills the message of Christ in the hearts and minds of all members of the Church. The Word of God guides the life of the Church so that it can proclaim the Word to others. Faith-formation programs, catechetical classes, small-faith communities and other such groups are all ways the Word is preached and shared. Both in proclaiming the Word to others and in living lives that are examples of gospel values, the Church shares the good news of salvation and evangelizes those who have not heard it.

Prayer and Worship

During his earthly life, Jesus prayed and worshiped. Thus, worship is the heart and soul of the Church. The eucharistic liturgy is the "source and summit" of our lives, as the Vatican Council Fathers taught. In the liturgy and sacraments, the mission of Christ is continued. The leadership within the parish—priests, liturgists, pastoral councils, pastoral ministers—is to strive to make worship worthy of its name by continued thoughtful attention to how it is done and how it can be improved. In this way, the Eucharist feeds, transforms, and challenges the members of the community.

Serving Others

Jesus served others and healed those in need. By his example, he taught us how to live as servants. In fact, the criteria he gave for our eternal happiness is a life of service: "Come, you that…inherit the kingdom prepared for you from the foundation of the world; for I was hungry and you gave me food, I was thirsty and you gave me something to drink, I was a stranger and you welcomed me, I was naked and you gave me clothing, I was sick and you took care of me, I was in prison and you visited me" (Mt 25:34–36). Jesus goes on to explain, "Truly I tell you, just as you did it to one of the least of these who are members of my family, you did it to me" (Mt 25:40).

Service is the hallmark of the Christian way of life, of the Church today. The Church is an instrument of service, both as a community and insofar as its individual members commit themselves to the service of others. The community members put themselves at the service of each other and, equally important, at the service of those outside the community.

Community

Just as Jesus gathered a community around him, the Church gathers its members so that they may experience the strength of the graced community and witness together as the Body of Christ to the world. Community is interesting in that it is both a goal of the parish as well as a result of the parish attending well to the Word, the worship dimensions, and the service dimensions of its mission. Community happens when people learn together and share the joys and sufferings of life, when they share their faith insights, when they join together in full, active participation in the liturgy, when they join together in service to others.

If this is what the parish does—continues the mission of Christ by proclaiming the Word, worshiping and celebrating the sacraments, serving those in need, and gathering as a community—we can easily see what the focus of its leadership must be. The parish pastoral council, as a leadership body, is charged with looking at how the parish is doing in carrying out this mission in these four ways.

Vision and Challenge

Jesus gave to those he led a vision of something more. As a leadership body, promoting Christ's vision is the role of the pastoral council in a real sense. This body works to develop the correct understanding of the mission of the parish and to formulate policies and recommendations so that the necessary directions for carrying out the mission are clear. As Pope Paul VI said, the mission of the parish pastoral council is "to examine and consider all that relates to pastoral work and to offer practical conclusions on these matters, so that the life and activity of the People of God be brought into greater conformity with the Gospel."

Role Clarity

The parish council is not the pastor. Rather, the council serves as an advisory board to the pastor by virtue of Canon Law (see Canon 536, §2). Thus, it stands to reason that if the parish council is to give advice to the pastor, it obviously needs to be well-informed about what is happening, what should be happening to fulfill its mission, and what needs to happen if the parish is to live out Christ's mission to the fullest.

Likewise, the pastor needs to be clear and explicit about what he needs and wants from the pastoral council, and the parish council constitution and bylaws need to spell this out. These documents need to be working tools that are studied by each new member of the council, and that, furthermore, the council as a whole periodically should review them every few years to see if they need any updating or additions. These documents should make clear the role of the council, the length of terms of office, and the type of work and time commitments expected of its members. Parishioners, too, need to be familiar with these documents so they understand the role and functions of the council that represents their interests. It is appropriate to conduct this review at the time of discernment/election of new council members.

Some councils try to manage the parish staff and become involved in trying to "supervise" the day-to-day operations. The fact is, the parish council is not in charge of the parish staff. This type of involvement is an indication of a lack of clarity about the council's leadership role that can lead to conflicts and misunderstandings that erode the effectiveness of everyone involved.

I once worked with a council who called me because of their frustration at being ineffective. One woman said that she wanted to be of service to the parish, but commented that her evenings could be spent in much better ways that would be more worthwhile. Among other things, the group could never get through their agenda; items invariably went unaddressed because meetings ran too long. After reviewing how their meetings were run and going over a recent agenda, we looked specifically at the proceedings from the last meeting—only to learn that the group had spent forty-five minutes trying to decide if the parish kitchen should buy a new popcorn popper! Very little else was accomplished at that particular meeting, resulting in a high degree of frustration. I learned in a short period of time that this was typical of their evenings together.

To begin generating a greater sense of effective service within this group, we reviewed the differences between policy (their job) and management (which was not their job). In addition, adopting a new, simple, but clear template for putting together their regular agendas ensured that inappropriate items never came to the group. We also reviewed a simple and clear method for running meetings, which kept those kinds of "time overruns" from happening in the future.

The Pastor

The pastor has the right and the duty to do what God wills: to care for the community, to lead it in a discovery of the truth, to gather together its members so that they might make the Lord present. In a normal relationship between pastor and parish council, pastors welcome consultation and new ideas on how to best plan and carry out the parish's mission. They consult their councils to ensure a well-planned pastoral program that is appropriate to this particular parish at this time. The pastoral-council approach is to make the best use of the gifts of the Holy Spirit that are present in the broader community—talents and insights and ideas that the council can have in a way that no individual alone can possess. The pastoral council is the designated body for this sharing and consultation.

The Vatican II Decree on the Ministry and Life of Priests, paragraph 26 states: "Finally, priests have been placed in the midst of the laity so that they may lead them all to the unity of charity…Their's is the task, then, of bringing about agreement among divergent outlooks in such a way that nobody may feel a stranger in the Christian community." And paragraph 27 reads: "The pastors then, indeed, should recognize and promote the dignity and responsibility of the laity in the Church. They should willingly use their prudent advice and confidently assign duties to them in the service of the Church, leaving them freedom and scope for acting. Indeed, they should give them the courage to undertake works on their own initiative. Many benefits for the Church are to be expected from this familiar relationship between the laity and the pastors…. Strengthened by all her members, the Church can thus more effectively fulfill her mission for the life of the world."

Although the pastor has the primary role of leadership in the parish and is held accountable for its well being, the laity are to assist him in whatever way possible. As one pastor told me, "How foolish I'd be not to welcome all the wisdom, thought, and advice I can get as we do pastoral planning! How foolish I'd be not to take the council's thoughtful and studied ideas seriously. How foolish I'd be if I disagree with them, not to take it seriously if I felt I had to override their consensus. How foolish I'd be not to explain my reasons for doing so. How foolish. And I'm no fool!"

The Parish Dance Floor

A council is a policymaking group, while others (committees, staff, volunteers) implement policies of the council. The council, a consultative body, neither legislates nor administrates. Rather, it develops plans and policies with the pastor. It doesn't direct other parish organizations. Sometimes councils struggle with the difference between policy and administration.

To help councils clarify their role in the parish, I often use the image of the balcony and the dance floor. Picture a large gathering, such as a wedding, where there is music playing and people dancing in various ways and in different movements around a large dance floor. At one end of the room is a balcony that overlooks all this activity. On the balcony are onlookers who are observing all the action on the dance floor. In this metaphor, the parish groups and various activities are on the dance floor. The role of the council, as a body, is not to be on the dance floor showing people a new step but on the balcony, looking at the big picture and assessing and imagining what might improve the next dance.

Of course, if council members are to effectively assess and imagine what might need to be improved, they need to constantly listen to and talk with parish members to hear their needs and their concerns. Through listening in various ways, the council articulates the vision and mission of the parish. Their job as a council is not to micromanage or interfere with ongoing activities, but to set policies and goals so that needs are met and the challenges of the gospel are addressed.

So the role of the council is that of a visioning body. It vigilantly watches the big picture and takes responsibility for pastoral planning and goal setting. The council paints a picture of what the parish could be if hearts were truly on fire with the gospel as it was for the disciples on the road to Emmaus. It then goes about painting that picture in the minds and hearts of every parishioner, seeing that the appropriate staff, committees, and organizations are aware of the goals and are taking action to implement them in their own planning and activities. Thus, although there is a great deal of activity, the dance is coordinated; all are dancing to the same music. The council is a monitoring body who sees that the goals are being appropriately implemented and that there is one vision for the parish—one vision that permeates all the ministries. The parish council sometimes divides up this monitoring activity and appoints committees to report regularly on how matters in their area are working. Thus, the council plans and sets policy, and the staff and committees are responsible for implementing them and for reporting regularly to the council on how this is working.

Most council members wear more than one hat in their role as a member of the parish. For example, a person may serve as a council member and, during that same term, serve as a volunteer in a group or a leader of an organization. I often remind council members to be aware of what hat they're wearing, and to change hats when they change roles. As a council member, however, they must support the decisions of the council in private and in public, no matter what "hat" they're wearing at the moment. They must also respect the agreed upon confidentiality of the council, especially in the case of alternate opinions and voices. In other words, when a council member is wearing a hat other than his or her "council member hat," that person does not join in criticism or gossip about council actions. Rather, council members support one another publicly and privately.

Pastoral Council As Community

Perhaps the most important role of the parish council as a body is to model the kind of community it envisions for the parish. Thus, parish pastoral council meetings should be unlike any other business meeting one might attend. This group is called to take on a role beyond governance and planning and policy formation. The group can do what it is called to do only when it provides a model of spiritual leadership. This assumes that a large part of each council meeting is spent in prayerful reflection—for example, taking the Scripture readings of the day, or an appropriate reading, and spending time sharing its meaning with one another. It also means examining each issue in the light of the gospel and the mission of the parish. It means making time during meetings, such as before making a decision on an issue to stop and to pray for guidance from the Spirit; it means connecting with each other as a community and offering prayer and support to each other. In other words, the council strives to *be* a model of what it is trying to move the parish toward.

Qualities Needed for a Parish Council

What kind of people make the best council members? The answer is easy. Good council members will possess two qualities. They are people who have big ears and people who are willing to learn. Big ears means that the person pays attention. He or she consciously and deliberately listens to as many voices and needs of parishioners as possible in order to bring those needs and opinions to the council table. It means that the person does not come with an agenda or to represent a constituency, but has ears to hear all the needs and to consider the common good—to represent *all* the people while standing on the balcony.

We can either limit council membership to people who know everything they need to know in order to be a councilor *or* we can chose people who are willing to take time to learn. Every council meeting should include some kind of ongoing education. In fact, I recommend that this be a regular part of the agenda and that there is a plan for what will be studied together over the course of the year. A book can be read and a chapter discussed each month; a speaker can be brought in for a brief presentation; a Church document can be studied; the parish constitution and bylaws can be systematically reviewed, and so on. Ongoing education also means learning how to be a prayerful person, a prayerful community, perhaps even learning to pray in new ways as a councilor. It means willingness to learn to be a discerner rather than just an advocator.

Persons who offer themselves as parish pastoral council members are generous souls. They are dedicated people who contribute enormous time, energy, and commitment to their community. They offer leadership—and they deserve leadership that will help them become the best pastoral council possible. Setting up, serving on, and implementing a vibrant parish council is an endeavor worth everyone's time and commitment.

Resources for Additional Reading

Bausch, William J. *The Hands-On-Parish: Reflections and Suggestions for Fostering Community.* Mystic, CT: Twenty-Third Publications, 1999.

Deegan, Arthur X., II, ed. *Developing a Vibrant Parish Pastoral Council.* Mahwah, N.J.: Paulist Press, 1995.

Gubish, Mary Ann and Susan Jenny, S.C., with Arlene McGannon. *Revisioning the Parish Pastoral Council.* Mahwah, N.J.: Paulist Press, 2001.

Hiesberger, Jean Marie, ed. *ParishWorks* newsletter, contains a regular column on Parish Pastoral Councils. Mahwah, N.J.: Paulist Press.

CHAPTER 7

Volunteers: Responding to the Baptismal Call

~

Tell me, and I will forget. Show me, and I may not remember. Involve me, and I will understand.

AMERICAN PROVERB

Healthy is the parish that has not a few people doing many things but many people each doing the things that they do best to build up the community. When we are baptized into a community, we come into a family of faith. And in healthy families, each person shares the responsibilities of family life to some extent. In a healthy parish, each person gives as well as receives. Many parishes, of course, promote the stewardship concept of each person contributing time, talent, and treasure. Ideally, members of the community give their treasure and offer their time and talent. They come to get as well as to *give* in some measure.

With parishes developing as centers of community life, and not just sacramental "filling stations," as some were viewed before the Second Vatican Council, they have become beehives of activity. With a comprehensive view of stewardship, which includes the offering of one's time and talent, programs and activities tend to increase, and more volunteers are needed to support these activities. Some parishes even have a Director of Volunteerism to coordinate these many functions, committees, and activities. Where do volunteers come from and how are they recruited and organized?

Recruitment of Volunteers

During the annual Stewardship Appeal, parishioners are asked to list several of the ways in which they can or will offer their talents. Likewise, when new parishioners come into the parish, they, too, are introduced to the notion and expectation of giving of their time to the community, and they are shown opportunities to become active members of the Church.

Some parishes have a booklet containing the parish mission statement and a list of all the activities, committees, and organizations, what they do, and the contact person(s) for each group. I recall visiting a diocesan cathedral parish where a table at the entrance of the church welcomed people and asked them to take a copy of such a booklet. It was both inviting and impressive to see the richness of the parish life in that faith community.

When Is Recruitment Time?

Recruitment is typically thought of as a summer activity, when folks are in their "down time" and many activities and meetings in the parish are on hold or a modified schedule. Since summer is also a good time for planning the next year's events and activities, volunteer recruitment is a natural adjunct. If groups function on the school-year model, they need to spend the summer months putting together the goals and plans that will be launched in the fall. In order to begin the new season in the fall, volunteers need to be recruited and perhaps even trained before the activities get underway. Groups that use the mentoring system, in which someone partners with another for a year before taking over a particular activity, will be looking for their prospective volunteers an entire year ahead. Many DREs, youth ministers, home visitors, and so on, use this model of having a new volunteer assist a seasoned volunteer for a year as a kind of apprentice system. Regardless of the system used, successful volunteer recruiters know, however, that it is important to take volunteer recruitment seriously *all year long*.

Committee Members Are Good Recruiters

Committee and group leaders need to regularly remind current volunteers of the need to search out and actively seek new members. In other words, recruitment is not the sole responsibility of the leader. Someone who is enthusiastic about, currently working on, and committed to a given project is an excellent person to invite others to join the effort.

There are many ways to recruit volunteers:

- Let your needs be known far and wide: Remind the parish staff of specific talents or kinds of people you want, and ask them for suggestions from their contacts. Put "Want Ads" in the parish bulletin. These brief but specific descriptions of who you need and what they would be doing are especially effective for one-time tasks or projects without an ongoing commitment. Ask people who turn down your invitation if they can suggest someone else you might approach.

- Collaborate: Talk with other parish leaders about your specific needs. They may have volunteers who are ready for a change or not really satisfied with what they are currently doing. Just remember to return the favor! Don't hoard your volunteers; rather, refer them to other parish ministries.

- Activity fairs: One weekend a year, each group that uses volunteers sets up a table or an area in the community gathering space. Then, after each Mass that weekend, people can move from one station to another in order to have the opportunity to obtain information about each of the organizations represented. Inquirers can pick up small, attractive handouts that describe a given organization, its mission and activities, and some specifics about what is needed from volunteers. Organizations can also arrange for current members to be on hand to answer questions directly. Members of the choir, for example, could be on hand to sing; some teens could be available to answer questions about the youth group and talk about what they've done together in the past. In other words, engage prospects and give them a taste or a feel both of the *people* currently involved and of the *activity* they'll help with.

The weekend following the "Activity Fair" is "Sign Up Weekend," when forms are passed out for parishioners to indicate what volunteer activity they are interested in supporting. These forms can be collected in the offering basket—it is as real and as important an offering as the collection envelope. Because there is an expectation that everyone does something, the readings and the homily during these two Sundays can reinforce this sense of stewardship. It is imperative that these forms—and all interests expressed by potential volunteers—are collected efficiently and the information passed on, so that all volunteers can be contacted within a matter of weeks.

• The Parish Welcome Committee: Work with the Parish Welcome Committee on how to integrate new parishioners. Be aware of the specifics of how new parishioners are welcomed and integrated into the parish community. I remember moving to a new parish, going to the rectory to sign up, and being ushered into the finance manager's office, where I was told what was expected of me financially if I registered a child in the parish school. A priest was standing in the adjoining doorway watching, but left without speaking before we finished. I met no one else and was given no other information about the parish. I did ask what time the Masses were on Sunday. When I returned home, still in a daze at the "welcome" I'd received, I found a note attached to a loaf of freshly baked bread left on my doorstep. The note welcomed me to the area and invited me, if I had no other church affiliation, to come to church on Sunday to worship. The note also included a schedule of services and events, and a handwritten note of apology expressing disappointment that I hadn't been available when the caller stopped by. At the bottom of the note, the man left his name and phone number. This warm and inviting greeting was from another denomination in the neighborhood.

A friend of mine described her experience of relocating and going to the parish office to register. Her pastor greeted her, visited with her and her family. He described the parish community, and he took the time to explain what the parish was trying to do and what it was trying to be, both for its members and for others outside the church. He then asked my friend how she saw her role in the community. When she said she wanted to sit back and watch for a while, the priest explained that that wasn't an option. "Everyone both gives and receives in some way," he explained. He next asked her to take time to look over the parish booklet and get settled into the community for a bit. Someone then would call and visit with her about how and where she would like to tithe her talents. In the follow-up meeting with a parish contact person, my friend felt that this parish representative was truly interested in her and her interests and in helping her find just the right place in the parish. They talked about my friend's past experiences, her talents and interests, and who could help her "network" into the parish. As this parish welcome visit concluded, my friend was left giving an indication of which place in the parish she would consider giving her volunteer time. The parish representative then had that committee leader contact the new prospect.

When her job moved her again in a couple of years, my friend was amazingly rooted and integrated in her parish. Her experience of being welcomed and of volunteering had both fed and nurtured her, as well as putting her skills, talents, and interests to use for the good of others. It's hard to "get into" a community, my friend said. "This was the best and richest of all my experiences." Some of the things she felt this parish had done well included:

- Helping her feel welcome on her first encounter, and connecting her with someone who could follow through with her. That person helped with both her volunteer placement and her social connections.

- Being clear about the goals and mission of the parish and the expectations of using her talents in the service of others.

- Focusing on her as a person, through personal contact, and tying her previous experience and her skills and talents to appropriate volunteer opportunities. Each time she was referred (from pastor to staff person to committee head), the person who contacted her was clearly interested in her as a human being, not just in "using" her.

- Giving her time to reflect on her decision, yet following up with her. One of the worst, yet most frequent mistakes parishes make is asking people to volunteer but not following up with them. One woman said, "Never again! I've signed up three years in a row for the food pantry, and no one has yet been in touch."

• Welcoming her ideas and skills. The members of the group she did join were open to a newcomer; they were not a closed committee that had been relying on the same people for years. They were welcoming and eager for her contribution.

Successful "recruiters" know that they cannot catch people on their way out of Sunday liturgy, tell them how desperate their needs are for volunteer help, and ask them to make a commitment on the spot. One volunteer coordinator says he may catch them on Sunday and ask if he can call to talk with them at a later time. He then phones that person and sets up a face-to-face conversation that includes the specifics of the job and the time commitment involved. He also tells prospective volunteers not to say either yes or no at that point, but rather to go home and think about it, talk with other family members, and pray over it. He then arranges for a second meeting to bring closure one way or another. This recruiter understands the importance of knowing people's reasons for saying no; if they do, it gives him helpful information for approaching others. He also uses this second meeting as a time to solicit a commitment from people to consider volunteering in the future, and to ask for recommendations of other people who might take on the job. He tries to remain gracious and affirming, regardless of people's final decision. "There's always tomorrow," he says, "and the goal is not to make people feel bad, but to help them feel they are valued in the community."

Matching Talents With Roles

Having the wrong person in the wrong position, whether volunteer or paid, does no one any good. In fact, the opposite is true: volunteers who are not well-suited for their jobs become frustrated, unhappy, and unfulfilled, and the work doesn't get done as it should. Others involved in the work can be negatively affected by the situation as well.

Thus, taking the time to visit with volunteers to "get the placement right" is well worth the time and energy at the outset. This should be done in a conversational manner, not as if you were in an "interviewing-and-hiring" process. Talk with prospective volunteers about what they've enjoyed doing in the past, what they like to do, and why they might want to do this particular job.

Do not recruit for meaningless work; rather, delegate significant jobs to volunteers who are qualified. Some people look for something where they can "stamp and stuff" but the recruiter needs to be clear that these routine tasks are what is involved.

No volunteer position should be without a role description. A one-pager can be very simple and straightforward, and should include information such as:

- the title of the job or the position, and the name, address, and contact information of the person to whom the volunteer is responsible;

- a description of the duties as well as the skills a person needs for this job, including how much time is required and when the job needs to be completed, if it is on a schedule;

- the length of the "term" of service;

- the training required for the job and the assurance that the individual will get that needed training;

- most importantly, how this volunteer work fits into the mission and current goals of the parish;

- finally, the rules of confidentiality involved in the job and, in this day and age, the possible background checks expected of any volunteers who will be working in sensitive areas, especially with children.

Once people volunteer to be part of an activity or project, take care that they are given an initial orientation; ideally, this will be conducted by an experienced person on the project team, but it is helpful to include a checklist that ensures all pertinent information is exchanged. For example, the volunteer's name, contact information, birthday, availability, work and vacation schedules, and so on, should be noted on a "Vital Information Form," and this form should be filed along with any notations about the volunteer's special interests, other requirements, or concerns. For example, a volunteer may be available only on certain days, have special child-care needs, or be away all summer every year. Volunteer orientation should also include a thorough review of the volunteers' responsibilities, including what to do and whom to contact if they can't fulfill a time slot, whether they are expected to secure their own substitutes, and so on.

Finally, brainstorm with current volunteers to be sure you have all the information newcomers to the committee will need or want. For example, be sure new recruits have a clear understanding of who oversees this committee or project, and how the project or committee fits into the overall parish organizational chart. It might be helpful to collect this information on a form that can be reviewed individually with each newcomer to the group.

Support and Appreciation

What is it we're trying to accomplish here? Is it to get a mission fulfilled? A job done? A sense of ownership and community enhanced? A stronger spirit of teamwork and accomplishment? Perhaps all of the above! Keeping your eye on what it is you are trying to accomplish is a key to effective volunteer management. What would *you* appreciate if you were giving time and talent as the volunteers are (and you no doubt are!)?

• Place: Provide a place where volunteer workers can carry out their tasks. One parish has established a Volunteer Room, complete with a well-stocked supply closet, a copy and fax machine, a computer and telephone, a large plain table to spread out work on, and a folding door that can be used to separate a space for a committee to meet while other projects are being carried out in the workspace. A small refrigerator and a microwave oven sit in the corner by a coffeepot. A basket of hard candies sits in the middle of the table and, more often than not, a plate of cookies magically appears—sometimes brought by staff, usually by volunteers. There is also a secure place for workers to hang their coats and jackets and leave purses and other personal belongings.

The environments we create say something about the importance of what is happening in that space and the importance of the people there. Even part of a basement can be spruced up by (of course!) volunteers, to make the space practical and inviting for that one-time project. Just making the effort to provide a comfortable environment—even if it's less than ideal—helps people feel good about what they're doing.

- Relationships: When new people join a committee or group, make arrangements to acknowledge and welcome them at the next gathering. Let them tell about themselves and why they've chosen to volunteer for this particular task. But welcoming is only the beginning.

There are so many seemingly unimportant ways to help people feel important and connected. Many groups, for example, have annual appreciation dinners, luncheons, or receptions, oftentimes scheduled for the holiday season or the end of the school year. At these celebrations, volunteers are often presented with a gift, such as a book related to their volunteering.

The following list includes other ways to appreciate, nurture, and encourage good volunteers. As you read, place a check (✓) next to the things you already do. Place an exclamation point (!) next to the things you want to begin doing.

- Acknowledge your volunteers when you meet them outside the group, be it at liturgy, the supermarket, or anywhere else you happen to cross paths.

- Send birthday cards to your volunteers; you know the date because you have that on their "Vital Information Form."

- When you see volunteers' family members, thank them for sharing the person with you, and compliment their work.

- Be considerate of your volunteers when they have special needs, such as changing their volunteer dates.

- Say thank you! And say it often!

- Involve your volunteers in planning for the future. Get their suggestions—and use them. Take time to gather, review how their ideas fit in with the overall goals of the parish, what you are all trying to accomplish together, and how things might be improved.

- Provide refreshments and, especially, whatever supplies are needed so that volunteers can complete their tasks.

- Facilitate the planning of any social gatherings your volunteers might be interested in, but do not be responsible for doing it all yourself.

• Help volunteers move on to other challenges rather than stay in the same "slot" indefinitely. Set up a meeting with another staff person or committee head in charge of a volunteer function for which they might be particularly suited.

What would you add to this list?

Training and Formation

Certain volunteer efforts can be greatly enhanced when ongoing training is provided. It should be assumed, for example, that parish pastoral council members, volunteer catechists, and liturgical ministers are provided with continuous formation. After all, who else could benefit from in-service workshops or events? This need not be an extravagant event or entail a great many resources. Inviting the leader of another organization to share his or her experience dealing with problems in the group is a simple way to support the ongoing training and formation of your volunteers.

Combining groups is also feasible and effective, such as inviting all heads of parish committees for an evening or two hours on a weekend to attend a presentation on How to Run an Effective Meeting. If you're a committee head, take your suggestion to your peers or a staff person. If you're a staff person, invite such a group to meet, and see what common help people could use.

What about approaching the pastor or council for funding to send key people to an outside workshop, if this opportunity is not currently provided? Not-for-profit groups often conduct seminars that provide usable suggestions for volunteer groups. If this cannot be arranged for the current year, ask about getting it included in next year's budget.

One common help we all need and benefit from is regular spiritual formation. How about an evening or weekend afternoon mini-retreat for all volunteers? Some parishes take the time to train all committee and group leaders to reflect on the Sunday Scripture readings, so they can make this reflection part of the regular meetings with their respective groups.

Evaluation

Evaluation is such a helpful part of any experience—but, unfortunately, it is the one exercise most often skipped. When we step back and look at how things are going, we offer ourselves the opportunity to celebrate our successes. This is affirming and energizing, and it deepens commitment for all involved. Evaluation also offers the opportunity to change things for the better, something most of us welcome when we're involved in that process. Changing things for the better also encourages and re-energizes us, and can get us back on track when we've wandered from our goals or mission.

Volunteers can be both helped and helpful in this process. Inviting people to talk with you about how things are going, what they had hoped to accomplish or experience from this experience of volunteering, and what suggestions they might have for improvement—their own or the group's—helps you gather the important information you need to do a valid evaluation and make constructive changes as needed. Sometimes there are needs that are simple to meet, and positive changes that are easy to make. One woman, for example, needed to change her volunteer schedule but wouldn't speak up until she was asked one to one for input about her personal volunteer experience. Another person suggested an entirely different system for printing labels—only to learn that the committee member who had been responsible for this task was completely burned out but didn't want to hurt the group's feelings by moving on.

Yearly assessment conversations can provide great opportunities for checkups, by the volunteers as well as the persons in charge. People can be asked to recommit to another year or to work with you to find a better or different place to use their skills. When you've observed that the job and the volunteer is not a good match, be clear, be sensitive, and be helpful to the person in locating a better fit. Encourage the use of talents you've observed and offer suggestions—and follow through with them in finding the right place and connecting them with the appropriate persons to make the change. New opportunities bring growth to the individual, to the position and organization they leave, and to where they go. In this process of change, it is critical for parish leaders to be in touch with one another. If you work with volunteers for teens, for example, and see someone is ready for a change or they're not able to provide what is needed, you can consider other skills you've seen that person exhibit. Perhaps you might have observed that person demonstrating strong speaking skills and a calm demeanor in large-group settings. Thus, you might recommend them for lector training, or perhaps for getting involved with the adult faith-formation committee. This kind of change benefits the individual *and* the parish community. Always try to walk with people toward the next stage, as much as they want and need.

When people move on—be it their decision or yours, and regardless of the reason—ask them to help you by providing an evaluation of their experience. The following form can easily be adapted to your needs. Even if you may want something simpler and more succinct, this form can serve as an initial template in the development of your own tool.

Report and Evaluation of a Volunteer Ministry

NAME _____ DATE _____

NAME OF MINISTRY/VOLUNTEER POSITION _____

TERM OF THE POSITION: FROM _____ TO _____

1. This ministry position has been satisfying for me because…
2. The major frustrations in this ministry position have been…
3. I used the following skills in this ministry position…
4. The training I received for this position included…
5. I felt supported in this position in the following ways…
6. I received the following resources which assisted me in this position…
7. I would have been able to do this ministry better if…
8. The highlights of this ministry for me have been…
9. The major accomplishments which have been achieved through this ministry include…
10. A person following me in this ministry position needs to know…

Please rate each of the following as it enabled you to do this ministry effectively and faithfully by placing an "X" where you feel it is most appropriate.

	Outstanding	Average	Inadequate
11. The way in which the position was interpreted and explained to me before I began.			
12. The training I received for doing the ministry.			
13. The support I received from the parish.			
14. The challenge and responsibility I felt in doing this ministry.			
15. The sense of importance the parish places on this ministry.			

The following are about your future volunteer ministries. Please indicate your interests by placing an "X" in the appropriate column.

16. Interest level in a new volunteer ministry:			
	Very Interested	Little Interest	No Interest
a. In my parish			
b. In my community			
c. In my deanery/diocese			
d. In an ecumenical setting			

17. Specific volunteer ministry opportunities I would like to explore include:

18. Factors in my situation that would influence my next volunteer ministry position are:

SCHEDULE: _____

TRANSPORTATION: _____

CHILD CARE: _____

OTHER: _____

A process of group assessment is another valuable tool for leaders of volunteer organizations. Like individual assessment, group assessment can have great benefits both for those involved in the work itself, and for the project or committee as a whole. At least once a year, gather the volunteers for an hour or two of guided assessment. During that time do the following:

- Review the goals for the year and the general goals and purpose of the project or committee.

- Have a brainstorming session to determine what has gone well, and have someone draft this list on newsprint. (Do not get bogged down in details or decisions.)

- Have a brainstorming session to determine what might have been done better, and have someone draft this list on newsprint. (Again, do not get bogged down in details or decisions.)

- Look at the big picture. Talk about the mission of the parish and the mission of the Church, and how the work of this group supports them.

- Clarify the coming year's goals. What should be done to strengthen and uphold the mission and goals of the parish? How can the group best accomplish this?

• Ask yourself these questions:

a. How are we doing with regard to comprehensive recruitment of volunteers?

b. What two things might we do to make recruitment of volunteers more effective?

c. How are we doing with regard to comprehensive recruitment of volunteers?

d. How might we improve evaluating the efforts of our volunteers?

e. Who else could I invite into a discussion of these above ideas?

Resources for Additional Reading

Bausch, William J. *The Total Parish Manual.* Mystic, CT: Twenty-Third Publications, 1996.

Hiesberger, Jean Marie, ed. *ParishWorks* newsletter, contains a regular column on Volunteers. Mahwah, N.J.: Paulist Press.

Ilsey, Paul J. *Enhancing the Volunteer Experience.* San Francisco: Jossey-Bass, 1990.

Pinsoneault, Donna. *Attracting and Managing Volunteers: A Parish Handbook.* Liguori, MO: Liguori Publications, 2001.

CHAPTER 8

Dealing With
Conflict and Anger:
Danger and Opportunity*

~

You do not lead by hitting people over the head—that's assault, not leadership.

DWIGHT D. EISENHOWER

I n a recent survey, pastors said that the major skill parish workers need help with is dealing with conflict and anger. While this survey result isn't surprising, it does underline the fact that conflict is a part of ordinary life, whether in the family, the workplace, the community, or the Church. Conflict exists because we are not all the same—and for that, we are grateful to God! How boring and uninteresting would life be otherwise.

The Chinese symbol for conflict is a combination of two Chinese words: *danger* and *opportunity*. This symbol provides a neutral label for conflict: conflict can be either positive or negative. Sometimes the most creative ideas and solutions to problems come out of talking through varying positions and viewpoints. Conflict can be an opportunity to better understand another person. Yet, the very same situation can result in people digging in their heels and labeling others negatively—or worse—

---

* Adapted from *Dealing With Conflict and Anger* by Jean Marie Hiesberger and Dr. William N. Hendricks, Overland Park, KS. National Press Publications, Inc., 1996, (800) 258-7248.

in respect to any future interactions. Conflict has possibilities in either direction. Everything depends, of course, on how it is handled.

What Is Conflict? What Is Anger?

Conflict might be defined as a battle, a disagreement, a difference of opinion or ideas, a misunderstanding. Think about how you would define the word "conflict." Whether it's between parish staff members, among parishioners, or within the family, neighborhood, or workplace, conflict most often centers around a difference of opinion—differences that are not always negative, but negative differences of opinion are often those that stand out most clearly in our minds.

Unlike conflict, *anger* is a feeling or an emotion. When that emotion is directed inward, it is *fear*. When it is directed outward, it is *anger*.

Why do we become angry? First of all, each of us naturally wants and needs to feel valued and loved—and from childhood on, we never outgrow this basic human need. We become angry when we feel we are not being valued as we should be and want to be.

Second, people become angry as a result of their need to be in control. A good deal our life is controlled by others. For example, we are controlled by the clock, by another's expectations, by schedules—sometime our own, and sometime the expectation of others. People in ministry are especially prone to having their lives scheduled by others, or by the calendar. Yet, we have a healthy need to control certain aspects of our lives at certain times, because always living under someone else's control is debilitating and intolerable.

A third basic cause of anger is the need for self-esteem. Feeling a sense of self-worth is the foundation for self-confidence. Fear or anger is a normal reaction when one's self-esteem is jeopardized, lost, or threatened. Interestingly, people with the greatest self-confidence are most able to control their anger.

Whether the emotion is directed inward and experienced as fear or directed outward as anger, we do have a choice about how we react to various situations. These emotions are ones which we can control and for which we can be held accountable. We have a choice about how we handle them. Simply put, feelings arise from our thoughts. We create our own thoughts, thus we can choose our feelings. While that is simple to say, it is not always simple to do. It requires reflection, determination, and practice. However, it can be liberating just to think of it in that way: we have a choice. Did you ever awake in the morning and look at the clock to find out if you feel tired or rested? Or perhaps you decided to laugh every time you encountered an inconsiderate driver, rather than feeling angry about it. You do control your anger and you do have a choice about it.

Others do not control your anger, you do. Others do not *make* you angry; rather, you make the choice to *be angry*. The good news is that just as you can choose to be angry, you can choose not to be angry. Understanding how this works will help you take responsibility for your emotions and control them. This is certainly not to say that you should never get angry. Even Jesus got angry, for example, at the merchants who were desecrating the Temple. Of course, it is easy to say that we can learn to choose our own responses. Perhaps if we understand the *why* and *how* of anger, this understanding can go a long way toward dealing with it positively.

Myths About Conflict

There are a number of myths about conflict that, when believed to represent the truth, simply make managing the conflict that much more difficult. Some of these are outlined in the paragraphs that follow:

• The presence of conflict must mean that there is poor leadership or management. Father Beckler is pastor of a medium-sized parish that employs several full-time and part-time staff members. Things usually go along pretty well in the parish, but Father sometimes wishes he knew how to manage people better because, from time to time, there is conflict among the staff and within the parish itself. *Maybe if I were a better manager,* he thinks to himself, *there wouldn't be so much conflict.*

This particular myth about conflict feeds on low self-esteem and insecurity. The fact is, conflict happens. It is sometimes possible to anticipate conflict, and to deal with conflict when it does arise. But conflict will still exist. As the saying goes, "Where two or three are gathered, there is conflict." But the presence of conflict is not a reason to shoulder the blame personally. Rather, learning about conflict and undertaking practice in dealing with it can help us relax and handle it.

It may appear that some settings are completely devoid of conflict. Not so. Where people interact regularly, there *is* conflict. A setting that appears to be without conflict simply means that the conflict is being managed and is not apparent to outsiders, or that the conflict is hidden and will eventually surface at a deeper and more serious level. The important thing is how the conflict is managed, not whether it is present. It is always present!

- The presence of conflict means people don't care. This conclusion is based on an assumption that people wouldn't fight and disagree unless they really didn't care. Actually, the opposite is often true. Conflict is the one way people indicate what is important to them. If we do not care about something, we are probably not willing to get into conflict about it. A staff person who gets upset about the way people are greeted when they phone the parish office indicates that hospitality is a value in the parish office setting. A parishioner who gets upset when the ministry to teens is discontinued displays a value to them for the faith formation of teens.

  Remember: Conflict can help clarify emotions and identify underlying values. Sometimes it is only when you are challenged by a situation that you discover how important it really is to you. Have you ever been surprised that you had such a strong reaction to something? That was your inner self revealing that this is something you care about more than you realized.

- In a conflict situation, anger is negative and bad. As mentioned previously, anger as an emotion is neither positive nor negative. Anger *can* be negative and destructive, of course, but it doesn't have to be. Rather, its impact is determined by what we do with it. Like conflict, anger can also be a sign of caring.

How anger is expressed is critical. Is it directed toward the person—or is it directed toward the problem? Is it channeled into positive problem solving—or is it used to fuel a sense of stubborn self-righteousness? Sometimes anger actually gives us the energy to mobilize toward a creative solution.

- Leave conflict alone and it will disappear. At best, this myth contains a half-truth. Indeed, we can avoid conflict—and sometimes avoidance is a valid strategy. But avoidance is not the *only* strategy, and is not always a *good* strategy to use. Conflict can escalate as easily as it can dissipate, but when it is not acknowledged, it may take on a life of its own. Ignoring conflict can allow it to grow out of proportion through gossip, innuendo, and inaction. Can you think of a time this happened to you?

- Conflict must be nipped in the bud. This strategy is obviously the counterpart to the previous myth. On the one hand, certain types of conflict will grow if left alone; however solving other types of conflict too quickly can mean you don't get the best solution. In this case, the underlying need is not problem solving but the desire to eliminate the unpleasant environment of the conflict as quickly as possible and restore at least the appearance of peace. However, if you slow down and take the time to define the conflict accurately and examine a variety of options, you will increase your chances of finding the best solution. A good rule of thumb is: conflict well-defined is a conflict half-solved.

Reflect on the following questions which may give you some insights into dealing with conflict.

- What are two ideas you found helpful in this information?

- What is one way you can use the information about conflict myths in your own situation?

- Think of a conflict situation you've been involved in. What insights do you have about it?

Managing Differences

Regardless of the group situation—be it ministry, family, or business—people realize greater success when they operate in a cooperative rather than an adversarial manner, when they help people learn to get along better with each other, and when they enable others to be more self-directed and self-motivated.

We know, however, that some people will continue to fight among themselves, that they will not get along with others, and that power plays still will occur. Here are some problem-solving rules to help eliminate infighting and to develop the kind of relationships that make for a happier, more Christian, and more productive work environment.

1. Attack the problem not the person. Have you ever come upon a parent and a child arguing in a public place? The parent is scowling at the child and scolding him in a loud voice, saying, "You're a bad, bad boy!" In another situation, you might hear two people arguing, one saying to the other, "If you weren't so lazy, you wouldn't always be behind in the schedule."

   These situations demonstrate the failure to distinguish between the behavior and the person. This response is both counterproductive and destructive. If you want effective communication, if you want behavior to change, if you want a problem to be solved, it is essential that you separate the behavior from the person. Whenever you have a problem with someone, you want to address the particular behavior, not that individual's personality.

   It would be far better for the parent to say to the child, "I don't like it when you scream in the store. If you can't speak in a quiet voice, we will leave." It would be more effective for the worker to say, "Let's look at how you're organizing your day. You're capable of handling this much work."

   Attacking people's character is never going to help change their behavior or attitude. Rather, it will simply make them more defensive—and a defensive person can hardly hear what another person is saying, much less be open to change.

2. It is better to describe your feelings than to act on them. There's a big difference between describing your feelings and acting them out. If you lose your temper, scream, or engage in name-calling, you are *acting out* your feelings. But when you say, "I'm upset because the building wasn't unlocked for the confirmation class," you're *describing* your feelings.

   When we have strong feelings, we usually want to express them. And when we express our feelings by defining them in a healthy and successful way—for example, "I'm frustrated that you haven't found a retreat director for our group yet"—we release our feelings in a way that is constructive. Allowing these kinds of feelings to smolder inside, however, will lead to their eventual eruption in a negative rather than a positive way. Not only will the "problem" not be addressed and handled, but a further barrier is created between ourselves and the other person with whom we are in conflict.

Defining our feelings as well as the specific problem—"I'm upset because the pastoral council wasn't told about this earlier"—shows that we are taking responsibility for our feelings. Additionally, it names the specific behavior so others are clear about what is upsetting us. In addition, when we make it clear that we are offering our perspective and not making a character judgment, others are free to offer their perspectives as well.

This kind of communication encourages open discussion and reduces defensiveness—especially when we're angry, upset, or frustrated. The less defensive everyone is, the more likely it is that the problem will get solved. This rule is a simple but important one, and it is not hard to follow—but it takes practice, especially if we have been communicating the other way for years!

3. Move from justification to resolution. Sometimes people get stuck justifying their position or behavior and defending themselves. In this kind of a problem situation, things can move quickly to pointing accusatory fingers at others. When problems arise and people begin to explain, excuse, or justify their behavior, move them quickly off that path toward the direction of defining and solving the problem. People are often so amazed to realize that the situation is not about blame that they will be glad to join in looking for a solution.

Many years ago, I was part of a team putting together a book by a well-known church leader. Somehow, when the book was finally printed, the author's name was misspelled on the cover! When our group was called into the manager's office, we were expecting heads to roll. Unbelievably, with the "offending" cover displayed on his desk, the manager began brainstorming with us about how we could adjust our processes so that this kind of error did not ever happen again. He had lots and lots of cooperation in that brainstorming session, you can be sure.

4. Look forward (to opportunity), not backward (for blame). A good rule is: No finger pointing, only solution pointing.

   There is something about human nature that instinctively wants to blame. In the Garden of Eden, for example, Adam pointed at Eve and said, "She made me do it." In day-to-day discussions, think how often we hear blame passed on to her, to him, to them, to the parishioners, to the full moon, or to anyone else. The mature person, however, wants to know how to improve, how to be more successful the next time. As Aristotle said, "An unexamined life is a waste of time."

5. Identify areas where you can give rather than take. A situation that ends with win/win results in a cooperative atmosphere, whether it's a family, a staff, a committee, or a council, and is a recipe for success. In your own mind, be clear about what you can live with or do without. Have an order of importance for your concessions in advance. Then, take one point at a time until each is agreed on to mutual satisfaction or, if not resolved, at least until there is agreement to table the point until a later time. Think ahead in any problem-solving situation and know your priorities. It's even a good idea to rank your priorities. What is negotiable for you? What is non-negotiable?

6. The angrier the event, the less likely logic will work. The more things heat up in a conflict, the more people stop listening. Simply put, anger breeds defensiveness. When you become defensive, you can no longer listen. Do everything you can to stay open, remain friendly—and do everything you can to help the other person to keep from becoming defensive as well. Otherwise, no one can hear the other person. A sincerely caring attitude or response can take the wind out of a person's sails like nothing else will!

But what if the wisdom of these rules does not bear fruit? If things do heat up, your role is to stay calm. Bring the discussion back to the issue at hand or, if that fails, calmly bring things to a close and agree to take up the issue at a specific time later.

The secret to dealing with conflict is learning what to do and then practicing, practicing, practicing. As you face your own challenges in dealing with conflict, ask yourself: *What one major thing do I want to practice doing differently when I next deal with conflict?* Consider discussing your answer with a confidant. Sharing a resolution and discussing how to keep it can clarify the resolution, deepen your commitment, and give you the added incentive you need to follow through. "Reporting" back to your confidant is also a helpful step. It provides an occasion to reflect on the experience and evaluate it, either to affirm how well you handled it or discuss why it didn't go so well and what to do next time.

What About Gossip and Backstabbing?

Gossip and backstabbing are behaviors that can demoralize people and seriously affect trust and productivity. An atmosphere where gossip exists separates people and results in hard feelings and conflict. As with so much in leadership and in dealing with conflict and anger, modeling by the leader is the most important teacher. This modeling means that you yourself refuse to listen to gossip, refuse to pass it on, and respectfully confront it when it happens. This is the major first step to take. Only when you stop participating in gossip yourself can you claim the right to confront gossiping in others.

Here are the three fail-safe steps that will help end gossiping:

1. When a person reports that someone is talking behind your back, ask that person to confront the gossiper with you. If gossiper's answer is yes, you've cut the gossip off and become accountable for finding the truth. Facing the gossiper will at best teach them that gossip is not part of the culture where they work and minister. At the least, it will keep them from gossiping to the two of you. Eventually, this spreads. If the gossiper's answer is no, then do the following.
2. Ask if you can use the other person's name with the gossiper and repeat what he said— then the other person is accountable for the information. If the answer to this request is no, go on to the next step. If the answer is yes, approach the gossiper in a manner that is not accusatory, but rather, searching for information. Ask the person if he or she did say what was reported. Let them give you their version of what they said. If they deny it, have them tell you why they think the other person might have said this about them. In any case, tell them why you do not want gossip to be part of the relationships on your team.

3. If the messenger will not allow you to use his or her name in confronting, say clearly and directly to this person, "Then this isn't true, and I'll do all I can to ignore and discredit this rumor." After that, most people will hesitate to come to you with gossip. This takes you out of the gossip loop or sequence in the future.

However, as a supervisor you need to distinguish between what is and is not work related. If it has nothing to do with work, you can simply respond, "I don't care to hear about this." If spreading gossip is affecting an employee's work, you need to confront the staff person. Communicate what you have heard and listen to the response. *Do not involve the person who came to you with the information.* Begin by asking open-ended questions. Listen to the response and explanation. Then decide how you need to handle the problem and end the gossip as soon as possible. Gossip will still go on but you'll stop it when it comes to you and you'll give chronic gossipers one less person to talk with. In addition, you will be making it clear that this behavior is something of which you disapprove.

On a separate piece of paper, write the personal resolution you want to make about gossip. It may be to stop listening or participating. It may be to confront a particular person the next time the gossiper comes to you, it may be to take action with an employee about whom you've been told some work-related information. Whatever you decide, be very specific in what you want to do and when you want to do it.

How to Talk About or "Confront" a Problem

Many conflicts are caused by poor communication. Sometimes lack of communication about a situation or avoiding a problem will itself cause a conflict. More often than not, however, the *style* of communicating is itself the problem. Poor communication can escalate anger and complicate the situation, which then becomes the source of another conflict.

Here is a simple technique for maintaining good communication in a conflict situation involving two people. It is a three-part-sentence method for communicating about a specific problem. The three parts of the sentence include: (1) naming the triggering event; (2) naming your feeling(s); and (3) naming the reason for your feeling(s).

Let's play out an example. When the parish secretary doesn't get the committee agenda prepared on time, you say: "Pat, when you don't have the agenda prepared on time for the committee meeting (sentence part 1), I feel frustrated (sentence part 2), because I can't lead the meeting properly without the agenda" (sentence part 3).

In part 1 of the sentence, you simply describe what happened ("When you do this" or "When this happens"). In part 2 of the sentence, you name the feelings *you* have about what happened ("I feel frustrated"). In part 3 of the sentence, finally, you give the reason for your feelings ("...because I can't lead the meeting properly without the agenda").

This simple three-part sentence is then followed by a statement such as "What I need is..." or a question such as "What can we do about this?" or "Can we talk about this?"—the intention being to seek resolution of the problem.

Let's look at some of the guidelines to keep in mind when using this three-part-sentence method:

- Describe the triggering event as concretely as possible, using specific terms, staying in the present, and never bringing up other issues. Keep this one single issue clearly in your own mind—even writing it down for yourself if you find that strategy helpful.

- Use "I" language and own your feelings. Say, "I feel," never "You made me feel."

- Avoid blaming language such as "You should have" or "You didn't...." The use of blaming language puts others on the defensive and probably creates greater conflict; it does not encourage resolution. Present the facts without judgment and avoid put downs and any second-guessing of the other person's motivations or intentions.

- Make a specific request. This means you need to be clear about what you want or need in this situation. "I need (want, would like, and so on)," for example, "to have them on my desk Wednesday morning before the committee meeting. If there's an emergency and you can't, I need you to let me know as soon as possible."

- Negotiate a solution without proving the other person is wrong or making the person feel bad. Keep your eye on the ball—remember that what you want or need out of this situation is a solution to the problem. Put downs, angry outbursts, blaming, and so on, are not going to get you what you need.

• Listen to the other person without interrupting. Although this guideline is not easy, it is an important part of helping the person feel like negotiating a solution rather than defending themselves, attacking you, blaming others, and so forth.

Here are three more examples of the three-part-sentence method of communication:

(1) When you return the car without gas in the tank,
(2) I feel nervous,
(3) because I have to take time to fill it unexpectedly and may be late to where I'm going.

(1) When you don't finish your meeting on time,
(2) I get frustrated,
(3) because my group and I are left standing in the hallway waiting for the room.

(1) When you don't give me my messages,
(2) I feel upset,
(3) because I discover a problem later and then get angry.

Practice this simple three-part-sentence method now. On a separate piece of paper, write the statements you would make about two situations in which this method would be helpful. First state the problem for yourself, then draft the three-part sentence, using the recommended format.

The Problem:

1. _____

2. _____

3. _____

The Problem:

1. _____

2. _____

3. _____

Although this method is simple, it can be difficult to put into practice, especially if you have been using other patterns of communication. It is often helpful to actually practice ahead of time what you are going to say, how you'll say it, and what you can live with as a solution. Resolution of a problem or conflict is worth the effort and frees you to focus your time and energy on things that are most important to you.

Conclusion

In parish life, as in all other areas of life, there is conflict. Using some of these insights will help us to be more effective in our roles in the parish. We have the added strength of being people of God, a people of faith who do not and cannot leave that dimension of life at the door. Because they are deeply held and connected to our ritual life and religious experience, religious issues are often the areas where there is great conflict. But we can, yes must, choose to at least try to be Christian in our dealings with one another.

This obviously does not mean avoiding or denying conflict. It does mean having a Christian manner of dealing with one another. It does mean allowing for the role of the Holy Spirit and being open to having our own mind and heart changed. It does means being willing to focus on the common good rather than on our individual wants or even needs. It does mean using the gospel as our guide, both in our decisions and in the methods by which we work toward agreement or consensus. It doesn't mean that it's easy—but it is important.

Resources for Additional Reading

Deutsch, Morton, and Peter Colemann, eds. *The Handbook of Conflict Resolution: Theory and Practice.* San Francisco: Jossey-Bass, 2000.

Hiesberger, Jean Marie and William N. Hendricks. *Dealing With Conflict and Anger.* Overland Park, KS: National Press Publications, Inc., 1996.

Keating, Charles J. *Dealing With Difficult People.* Mahwah, N.J.: Paulist Press, 1984.

Mayer, Bernard. *The Dynamics of Conflict Resolution: A Practitioner's Guide.* San Francisco: Jossey-Bass, 2000.

Stone, Douglas, Bruce Patton, Sheila Heen, and Roger Fisher. *Difficult Conversations.* New York, Penguin Books, 2000.

CHAPTER 9

How to Run a Meeting: Toward Positive and Productive Events

~

The most important thing a captain can do is to see the ship from the eyes of the crew.

PACIFIC FLEET COMMANDER D. MICHAEL ABRASHOFF

For many parish leaders, "attending meetings" is high on the list of "least favorite" activities and tasks. When asked why this response is so prevalent, typical answers include: "Too many," "Too long," "Waste of time," "Poorly run." And yet, we keep having them. For some people, meetings are considered the necessary evil to get things done, to involve people in decision-making and activities, and to do planning for projects and programs. But meetings don't have to be painful, dreaded experiences.

We have all attended meetings that started late and ended well past the designated (and productive) hour; that involved one person dominating the proceedings; that left us feeling like nothing was accomplished; that included pressure to decide something without sufficient information; that involved two factions arguing the time away. Hopefully, not all of these occurred at the same meeting!

Good leaders of meetings are not necessarily born with strong leadership skills. Rather, they have learned some simple, basic skills that help them facilitate and keep focused on the task at hand. By the same token, poor meetings are not necessarily the result of poor leadership. Many meetings are facilitated well but still prove to be inefficient, due to lack of clarity and lack of planning.

The following simple suggestions can help make meetings the positive and productive events they should be, can be, need to be!

Planning, Facilitating, and Closing

An effective meeting involves advance planning, good facilitation, and solid closure.

Advance Planning

- Be clear about the purpose of the meeting. Don't hold a meeting without a reason.

- Prepare a written agenda with time allotments for each item. Never put an agenda together at the beginning of a meeting because it wasn't done ahead of time. Rather, develop a system by which people know whom to contact to put items on the agenda, and what the deadline is. (More on planning the agenda on page 97.)

- For groups such as a pastoral council, members should receive the agenda several days before the meeting. In these days of electronic mail, this pre-notification is not an unreasonable expectation.

- For groups such as council or finance committees, where there is written material to be discussed, have the material to all members *well in advance of the meeting.* Be sure the material is clearly presented. Members need to read all pertinent material before the meeting, understand it, and come prepared to react to it, not to learn what it is.

- Attend to the meeting space. The arrangement and conditions of the room speak to the value of what the group is doing and to the importance of the attendees. Rotating responsibility for arranging the room, bringing refreshments, and so forth, can ensure this is done well.

• Start on time. End on time. Again, this practice is an indication of respect for attendees. If you wait for stragglers, the group eventually will get the message that you're not going to start on time, and will arrive accordingly.

Good Facilitation

• Integrate prayer into the meeting. Avoid "bookend" prayers, in the sense of perfunctory short prayers to begin and end the meeting. Be sure the prayer relates to the group and to the task at hand. This responsibility can be rotated among group members. Many groups, especially councils, use the Sunday or daily Scripture readings, and include a time for reflection and discussion.

• Review the agenda and time parameters at the beginning of the meeting. If it turns out that a topic is taking longer to discuss than expected, negotiate with the group for a specific added time to the meeting. Or, if more discussion or information is needed, carry the item over to the next meeting.

• The person chairing the meeting should be capable of handling the task. Some parishes hold periodic "training" sessions for committee heads, presidents of organizations, and anyone else interested in "how to run a meeting." The person facilitating needs to be capable of "reigning in" those who dominate and "bringing out" the quiet ones, while keeping the atmosphere pleasant and friendly.

• Appoint a timekeeper who is not the chairperson. That person can be helpful in moving things along. This task can be easily rotated within the group.

Solid Closure

• Review what has been accomplished and any decisions reached.

• Remind the group of decisions requiring follow-up action. Be sure the group understands *who* is to do *what* by *when*. Also, be sure participants know when they will receive minutes from the meeting.

• Review the time and place for the next meeting.

• Take time to assess together how the meeting went.

The Agenda

Different kinds of groups have different meeting needs. Some groups require regular, ongoing schedules, materials available for review beforehand, considerable discussion time of the material during the meeting, consensus for major decisions, and subcommittees or task forces for specific jobs. Other groups have "low-content" meetings or occasional meetings of a semisocial nature. Regular staff meetings, for example, involve complex purposes, including team building, time in shared prayer, coordinating calendars, as well as discussion and decision-making related to agenda items.

However, all groups have in common the need to feel that their time is well spent. They don't want the meeting controlled by an outspoken person while the agenda goes ignored and the chairperson seems helpless to do anything about the situation.

Here is a sample agenda for a group such as parish staff or council that meets regularly:

Date:

Chairperson:

Prayer:

Rounds: *(Each person has the opportunity to comment about what's going on with him or her personally.)*

Review of minutes from the previous meeting:

Information sharing: *(This is the time to share information about what each person is working on, upcoming events, follow-up to previous reports, and so on. Details that the group needs to be "informed about" are presented here.)*

Discussion and problem solving: *(Agenda items are discussed but no decisions are made. This is the time for members to solicit advice or do brain-*

storming, but decisions are made individually or with a committee at a later time. This is also the time to discuss matters that will require decisions at a later date. Perhaps more time is needed to reflect or get additional information in order to make an informed group decision later on.)

Decision-making: *(Here is where decision-making items belong. Perhaps these items were discussed at a previous meeting and are now on the agenda for a decision to be made. Perhaps they are being brought up for the first time here and decisions can be reached because further study is not required.)*

Next meeting: *(This is the time to set the date, agenda items, leadership tasks, chairperson, secretary, and prayer leader for the next meeting.)*

Making Decisions in a Group

There are a number of ways decisions can be made within a group setting. Two things are important in deciding which method to use. First, be sure everyone in the group understands which method is being used. If people are being asked to give advice and they think they're making the final decision, they will be frustrated and maybe even angry with the leader. Second, be sure to use a decision-making method that is appropriate to the decision and the circumstances.

Authority Rule, Authority Consults, Majority Vote, Minority Decides, Expert Makes Decision, and Consensus Decision-Making are among the most reliable methods for decision-making within a group.

- Authority Rule: The person with the most authority makes the decision. This is an especially useful method to employ when time is short and the decision to be made is fairly routine. It is sometimes used if the group doesn't have the necessary skills to make a particular decision.

- Authority Consults: The person responsible for making the decision asks the group for its input. The advantage, obviously, is that the wisdom and experience of the group is integrated into the process. This method of decision-making also helps members feel involved; people know they've had their say and their point of view was considered regardless of the outcome.

• Majority Vote: This method is much weaker than consensus because there are winners and losers. Thus, there is less commitment to the decision. However, this method is especially useful if the matter is not of great importance and if member commitment is not essential. It is sometimes used in the interest of saving time. That alone is not a good criteria, however.

• Minority Decides: The minority is usually an executive committee. This method is used when there is a time pressure and when it is not important to have a broad commitment. Sometimes it is used when only a few people have the needed skills or resources with which to make the decision. However, it can leave some people resentful, and unresolved conflict may linger within the group.

• Expert Makes Decision: Use this method of decision-making when one member of the group has an expertise in the area. Sometimes, of course, the challenge is in agreeing on who is the expert!

• Consensus Decision-making: This more complicated and time-demanding method is an important one to have in the repertoire of decision-making methods. Using this method assumes that all members fully understand the reasons for reaching a given decision and the details of the decision being made. It also assumes that all members are willing to support the decision. It provides the highest level of group commitment to the decision, as everyone has agreed to at least support it. This is the method to use when the decision to be made is especially important or complex. It demands the group's time, energy, and commitment to the process in advance.

Unlike voting and reaching a decision by majority, the consensus decision-making method leaves everyone a winner; there are no losers. Thus, there is a high level of commitment to the outcome. It also makes full use of all available resources. In the process of discussion, conflicts are immediately evident and resolved. The end results leave each member completely supporting the decision and understanding the reasons for reaching that particular decision.

In using this method, preparation is the key. Any relevant background information is made available to all group members, allowing for sufficient review and study before the decision is made. Once the item to be decided has been presented to the group, each person states his or her position and reasons for that position. No one is allowed to "pass" or "decline comment" because each person's insights, wisdom, and perspective are his or her essential gifts to the group. Each person actively listens to all others and is open to their own view being altered. There is no comment or reaction to anyone's opinion at this stage.

Once everyone has commented, open discussion is held for the purpose of surfacing new ideas, challenges, questions, and observations. This is a time for exploring for the best outcome, rather than arguing for a position. Differences are considered helpful to the process and a way of cultivating a richer understanding of the issue.

Everyone listens for a movement toward consensus. When it seems to be coming, the chairperson tests to see if there is a conclusion that all can support. This doesn't mean everyone will have high enthusiasm for the decision, but everyone will be able to at least support the decision publicly and privately. Agreement is not given simply to avoid conflict.

If there is not yet a conclusion that all can support, the discussion is reopened and continued until a consensus is reached. In a stalemate, the precise problem area is identified, and the group searches for the most acceptable alternative. Again, the end result should be a decision everyone in the group can at least "live with" and completely support, both privately and publicly. The final step in the consensus decision-making method is to review the process with the group.

Again, this is an important method to use for serious, important, and major decisions. It is important for several reasons. First, unlike voting, there are no losers. Thus there is a high level of commitment to the outcome. It also makes full use of all the available resources. In the process of discussion, conflicts are resolved. Each individual is able to support the decision and the reasons for supporting the decision.

Conclusion

There are a variety of reasons for meetings, and a variety of groups holding meetings. Good meetings have the additional benefits of connecting community members and of solidifying commitment to the parish projects and activities. Every person attending a meeting is responsible for making it a "successful" meeting. Each member needs to arrive at the meeting on time and be willing to contribute his or her ideas and opinions. Furthermore, each person's commitment goes beyond the room to support the activities of the group in every possible way. A well-run meeting helps to ensure that this will happen.

Resources for Additional Reading

Bausch, William J. *The Total Parish Manual: Everything You Need to Empower Your Faith Community.* Mystic, CT: Twenty-Third Publications, 1996.

McKinney, Mary Benet. *Sharing Wisdom: A Process for Group Decision Making.* Chicago: Thomas More, 1998.

CHAPTER 10

Change and Transition: Dealing With the Inevitable

∾

Lord, grant that we may always be right, for thou knowest that we will never change our minds.

OLD SCOTTISH PRAYER

Change happens. In fact, it sometimes seems that the most unchanging thing in life is that change happens. Things don't stay the same, no matter how much we wish for or work to resist change, toward maintaining that which is familiar, routine, and predictable. Life often seems more about living with change itself, rather than dealing with any change in particular.

Sometimes change is self-imposed; we choose it. For example, we might choose to sell the house and move to one that is larger or smaller. We may decide to switch jobs, join a new group, enroll in a class. At other times, change is imposed on us; we do not choose it. We get a new pastor. The city decides to make our one-way street a two-way thoroughfare. We are given a promotion. We fall and break our leg.

Finally, there are the changes that life passages bring. Our child is born and life changes dramatically. Someone we love dies. We (or perhaps our youngest child) leave the parental home. We reach retirement. Each stage of life brings change.

Personally, communally, and institutionally, we live in the midst of change every day. It has been said that the only person who really likes change is a baby with a wet diaper. Yet, some changes seem easier to manage and some individuals and groups seem more adaptable to change.

Review your attitude toward change by answering the following questions:

- What is a change that has occurred in your personal life in the past year?

- Which of the three categories does that change fit it into (chosen, imposed, life passage)?

- On a scale of 1 to 6, how easy has adjusting to this change been for you?

Piece of Cake! 1 2 3 4 5 6 Long way to go!

Change and Transition

According to William Bridges, who has written and lectured on transition for many years, all changes, personal or institutional, chosen or imposed, share common elements or phases. Bridges talks about the difference between "change" and "transition" as being a significant factor in understand as well as coping. Although they are two quite different things, we often equate them. But our doing so makes handling the process more difficult.

There is a big difference between change and transition. On September 11, 2001, a dramatic *change* happened for many people, but months and years later, the *transition* or adjustment to the change still continues.

Change, Bridges explains, happens when something starts or stops in our life. This can happen in an instant or over a short period of time. Change, for example, is an event such as a death, being fired, moving, hiring a new liturgist, winning the lottery. When change occurs, some circumstances of our life are different compared to the way they were before the change.

Transition, on the other hand, is not a starting or stopping *event*; it is a slow process. Transition is not something external; rather, transition is what happens inside us because of the change. It is *how* we deal with and adapt to change. Transition is psychological and involves a gradual "letting go" of how things were and becoming "at home" with the way things are now.

The Helpful Role of Ritual

Some people adapt more easily to change and some changes obviously demand more of us than others do. There are some things that can aid us in that adjustment. One of those things is to ritualize the ending stage. In our faith, we are so fortunate to have a rich treasure of rituals to draw upon. Our liturgy, for example, is the archetype for respecting and experiencing the power of ritual action. Ritual actions are a key factor in helping us with transitions. Merging parishes frequently pray, sing, and process, carrying of articles from one church to the other. One inner-city parish carried ritual books, oils, the tabernacle, and other significant articles through the neighborhood while they sang and danced to the accompaniment of trumpets. They wept and prayed and feasted and told stories to mark the ending of what had been. Together they wove a banner to symbolize the past, and that it was over.

Parents sometimes mark the key changes in their children's lives (and thus the family's) with rituals. Getting a driver's license, going off to college, changing schools—all endings and beginnings, these transitions can easily and meaningfully be marked with ritual. One family leaving their home of many years drew pictures of memories they had of the house and shared them. Then the young children went outside and gave a good-bye hug to the tree they played under. Neighbors had a farewell party for them. A hospital that merged departments made key rings from the old name tags for the staff and organized a "parade" of moving files, computers, and so forth, to new locations. A parish school that was being torn down to build a larger one held a big bonfire to destroy pieces of the old structure to ritually mark the ending. Telling stories at wakes is another form of ritual. We gather, we remember, we tell the story, we share our laughter or tears, perhaps we sing, and we share food. Ritualizing beginnings and endings does not need to be complicated, but it is helpful and significant in the psychological process of letting go and moving ahead.

Stages of Transition

Transition, Bridges explains, has three stages: the ending, the neutral time, and the beginning.

The Ending

Something begins: a new job, a medical treatment, riding in a different carpool, beginning a diet, starting high school, taking the youngest child to the first day of school. At the same time, something stops being the way it was, the way we knew things to be. One day there are two priests staffing our parish and, on the appointed day, there is just one. But with these beginnings, something ends. One day we are a single person and the next day we are a spouse. A stage has ended. One day we are childless and the next day the adoption agency brings us twins. Something has ended—like uninterrupted sleep. Good or bad, chosen or not, the ending piece needs to be acknowledged.

Neutral Time and Beginning

The next phases of transition, neutral time and beginning, happen in the opposite way of the ending. The transition phases of neutral time and beginning happen slowly and over a period of time. Our adjustment to the ending phase doesn't happen abruptly and on an appointed day. Rather we go through a beginning time and a neutral phase where we live through the psychological adjustments the change requires. Futurist Marilyn Ferguson describes these phases as being as being similar to swinging from one trapeze to another. We have let go of the first trapeze but we don't yet have the second in our grasp. We've let go of the "old" but are not yet truly part of the "new"—and there's nothing to hold on to. We are in a place of "living into the new," even if the passage is a chosen and happy one. The beginning phase and the neutral phase are often filled with uncertainty, discomfort, and sometimes resentment or anger.

Neutral time is perhaps what it was like for Moses and the Israelites during the forty years they spent in the desert. They had left their home and were not yet to the promised land. They were in the neutral time. A person who is stuck "in betwixt and between," for example, a person bitter about an "unfair" blow life has dealt can be in the neutral zone for a long time. Even someone who is grieving the death of a beloved spouse and is working through that grief in the healthiest way possible can spend a long time in this phase or stage. We sometimes live in the neutral part of a transition for a long time, but sometimes this period is much shorter. There are many variables that influence how long one spends in neutral time.

Bridges describes four things that can help us move through the in-between neutral time: control, understanding, support, and purpose. Hanging between trapezes, one can feel like everything is out of control. Rarely is that actually the case. Taking time to name the things that remain in control can be helpful. Articulating these to a group in transition is important—just what things will *not* change? What decisions *do* you have control over?

Doing everything possible to explain and to understand the why and the how of a change is another bonus. For many people, making sense of what's happening puts them greatly at ease. Otherwise, speculating, gossiping, and misinterpreting all get in the way of accepting and adjusting to a change.

Supporting one another in change and transition means that even if we are going through the process alone, we don't feel totally alone. In a personal transition, this can mean leaning on your prayer group or just spending more time with close friends whether or not you're talking explicitly about the transition you are going through.

Another thing that helps us walk this path of adjustment is to keep the purpose (the "why am I doing this?") in mind. Reminding ourselves and anyone involved over and over of the purpose of this transition as well as focusing on the overall purpose of the organization or group or parish helps everyone keep their eye on the ball, so to speak.

The beginning stage is when we have moved on and "lived into" the routines demanded of us when we face change. A beginning stage might be exemplified by the Jews settling into their new land after their desert experience and forging a new life and new routines. For example, the beginning stage might be seen as the adaptations made by a parish after it has "lived through" the situation of having only one priest on staff. It is the day when it seems as if we've always had twins in the house and are used to living with them.

The beginning, the *real* beginning, is when we are at peace, at home with whatever the change brought with it. Be patient with yourself and with the group that may be involved. Besides these practical suggestions, always remember to pray for patience, understanding, wisdom, and God's help through it all.

Look at the following questions to help you assess how you are dealing with change:

- In what transition are you still on the first trapeze?

- What will help you with the "control, understanding, support, and purpose" elements that Bridges names?

Ten Ways to Successfully Facilitate a Group Change

The following guidelines for and facts about change will help you be effective as a leader of change with a group such as a pastoral council, committee, parish community, and so on.

1. Carefully examine the *purpose* of the change. Change is not an end in itself. Ask again, What is our mission and how does it support the mission of Christ? The purpose of change in a ministry setting is simply *to bring about the mission through more effective ministry.* Is that the motivation? How will this change support that mission or purpose? Make sure the reason for and purpose of the change is true to it.

2. Realize that in the general population the number of those resisting change will far outnumber those enthusiastic about it. That is a given. Failing to acknowledge that the majority of people resist change makes for frustration as well as mistakes in strategy.

3. Most resistance to change is due to fear of a change in relationships. Many parishioners, for example, when told their parish will no longer have a resident priest but rather a lay pastoral administrator, can't imagine that the relationship with the larger Church will not be threatened. They fear that their parish will not be equal to others in the diocese. They do not want to give up their relationship with the priest, even if he is serving in several parishes and is not able to be

fully present. The relationship feels threatened. (In reality, these fears are usually unfounded.)

4. The intensity of resistance to change is in proportion to the threat to what people value. In other words, the degree to which people resist change can be an indication of their values. Whatever people hold as more important is what they are going to cling to and fight to retain. As a leader of change, you make a serious mistake when you fail to address such things directly.

5. In any group, people will fit into three categories: those who enthusiastically embrace a change, or the early adaptors; those who will come along eventually, the late adaptors; and those who, no matter how well-crafted the process, will never accept the change, never adapt. The late adaptors require the most energy. They will constitute the majority of the group, and will need to have their concerns heard and addressed, probably repeatedly.

6. Sociologists identify four factions within a group: the Innovators, the Opposers, the System Leaders, and the Rest. While the Innovators, or enthusiasts, will support the change, it is good for you, as the leader, not to identify with them too closely. Others in the group may perceive these enthusiasts as "oddballs" and resist what you and they want, based solely on that perception.

The Opposers will continue to be against the change, some forever. While they need to have your empathy and your ear to listen, it is probably futile to try to bring them around to acceptance.

The System Leaders are the key to broad-based acceptance. These are the informal leaders of the group. Many will look to them for their cue as to whether to accept the change or not. If the System Leaders are in favor of something, a host of others will not offer resistance.

Take the time to name for yourself who the people are in each of these factions. They may or may not be persons in formal leadership roles.

7. Planned change is usually effective in relation to the degree of input and involvement people have had in the process. In the long run, the time and patience required for a broad level of involvement is more than worth the effort. As one pastoral council leader said before introducing a major change, "We need to fill up not our gas tanks but our 'patience tanks' before we undertake this."

8. One of the key principles people find effective in introducing change is to start by strongly and effectively presenting the problem or the *need* for change. The temptation is to present the change or the solution itself. Selling the problem, so to speak, is more likely to get people on board with searching for a solution. They will then be ready to accept a change, even if it's not exactly what they proposed. They will also be more inclined to help get others enthusiastic, or at least accepting, and to support implementation of the solution.

9. As the leader, you will also need to be flexible and open to other ideas. This is true even if others have thought things through carefully and feel they know the perfect solution and plan for change!

10. In making a major change in the life of a community, people need certain things throughout the three stages of presenting the problem, facilitating consultation to determine a solution, and implementing the change. First, of course, they need to feel listened to, really heard. Then there is the need to be kept informed of where things are in the process. Finally, having a sense that things are progressing forward helps maintain continued support and with the transition adjustment. This last piece can be accomplished through a communications committee whose purpose is to continually apprise people of what's happening.

When implementing a major change, it is helpful break down the process into stages. Follow this up by reviewing and acknowledging publicly the completion of each stage. Then, as each stage is completed, celebrate, and review the next one. This helps people feel something is happening, even if it's not apparent. Sometimes, such as in a construction project or a major reorganization, there are long periods of time when things are happening but nothing is physically or publicly apparent. The community can be patient during these times if it is kept informed.

Here are some questions that may help you assess your "appetite" for change:

• Which of these ideas about change and transition do you want to share with someone who can help make change happen?

• Why would this idea be particularly helpful in your situation?

• Who do you want to talk with about this, and when will you contact that person/those persons?

Conclusion

Unless faced with an emergency situation, seasoned leaders of change know not to act alone. Rather, they utilize a broad-based leadership group or committee that works together to devise a well-thought-out process. They involve many others in carrying out the necessary steps in the listening and planning processes. Experienced leaders of change say that, at every step in the process, it is better to err on the side of too much information sharing rather than too little. They especially talk about the importance of praying privately as well as publicly with everyone involved, so that each step is under the care of the Spirit as well as human skills.

Resources for Additional Reading

Bridges, William. *Managing Transitions.* Reading, MA: Addison-Wesley, 1993.

Markham, Donna J. *Spiritlinking Leadership: Working Through Resistance to Organizational Change.* Mahwah, N.J.: Paulist Press, 1999.

Rendle, Gilbert. *Leading Change in the Congregation.* Bethesda, MD: Alban Institute, 1998.

Sofield, Loughlan and Donald Huhn. *The Collaborative Leader:* Notre Dame, IN: Ave Maria Press, 1995.

Self-Care and Personal Development of the Minister: Striking a Balance

⁓

Success is not the key to happiness. Happiness is the key to success.
If you love what you are doing, you will be successful.

HERMAN CAIN

Responsibility for ourselves is our first and primary responsibility in life. When we care for ourselves, we care for the primary responsibility that God gave us. When we care for ourselves, we are much better prepared to care for others, to reach out to our neighbors, to be productive members of our own family, our community, our society, and to live the gospel more fully along the path where our life takes us.

To everything there is a season, Ecclesiastes tells us, a time to be born, to die, to plant, to reap. Life changes. Seasons pass. The body is strong and then gradually, not so strong. The energy is boundless, then it lessens. The dreams and goals develop and modify. The cycle of life, indeed the cycles within life, make for constant change and surprise, even within certain stages of predictability. One thing that doesn't change, however, one of life's constants, is that to be healthy one must keep balance in life. Health doesn't happen for us or to us. Rather, it happens to the extent that we deliberately plan and make it happen.

Balance in life includes:

- being responsible for our physical health;

- taking time to be alone;

- caring for our social needs by taking time to be with others in various ways;

- making prayer and reflection an integral part of ordinary days;

- renewing ourselves through avenues such as nature, hobbies, journaling, volunteering, and so on.

Most people find that they have to *make* time, deliberately schedule time, to renew themselves within their ordinary days and in the places they normally live and work. This is primarily where we need renewal—the ordinary flow of life that takes its toll in large and small ways.

Physical Well-Being

A woman came up to me after a workshop and said that she had just completed a diet, had lost twenty-five pounds, and was now on a regular exercise regimen and eating more healthily. When I asked about her motivation, she said she had heard a sermon about the Holy Spirit. This was a new angle to me so I inquired further. In this homily, the woman said, the preacher had described the great gift that the Holy Spirit is to us, as a community and as individuals. The Holy Spirit is the fulfillment of Christ's promise to be with us always. The Spirit is with us in the church body, and in each one of us individually. In fact, the homilist said, our very bodies are temples of the Holy Spirit. "What kind of a temple do I want the Holy Spirit to dwell in?" she asked herself. "I'd be so upset if our cathedral or parish church were in disrepair and not worthy of God's presence. What about this temple!" The woman said she used that homily for her meditation for the next few days. As a result, she went for nutrition counseling and was in the process of changing some lifelong eating habits. She had successfully completed the first steps toward a more balanced life, she said, and was going to keep moving forward.

Caring for the temple of our body includes giving it proper rest, putting healthy food and other things into it, and giving it the exercise it needs for long-term sustenance.

- Which parts of my physical self-care am I doing well?

- Which do I need to improve?

- What will I do today or within the next week to help myself take a first step toward better self-care?

Take Time to Be Alone, Pray, Reflect

Martin Luther is often quoted as saying: "I have so much to do today that I'd better spend an extra hour in meditation this morning." While this may seem both contradictory and physically impossible, there's a great truth there. We need regular time to be quiet, to ask God's help, and to reflect and pray. We need it all the time but mostly when it's hardest to fit it in. The opportunity may not be there in *hours* of time, but the time *is* there, and each of us can find it.

One mother has two neighborhood teens stay with her young children for one hour after school one or two days a week. Sometimes she gets in the car and drives to the neighborhood park to sit and pray. Sometimes she takes a walk or goes to the bedroom and closes the door. What she does isn't as important as the fact that she does it *alone*. It is an important time for her.

Others find getting up a little earlier in the day, when the world is still quiet, allows them to enjoy the alone time they need. Some people use the time they're on "hold" on the telephone for brief snatches of prayer. Some take their lunch away from others at the office and use that as their reflection time.

Serena is a single mother with a ten-year-old daughter, Allyson. Serena has a responsible job and works hard. Her days are filled with meetings, phone calls, and people popping into her office for help and consultation. By the end of the day she often feels drained. "I need time," Serena says, "to unplug from the day, to process my day, and to switch back to my personal life before I can be a good mother to Allyson." She has learned that if she doesn't take time for herself she can't be really present and attentive in her role as mother.

Serena and Allyson have created a routine that allows each of them to have "decompression" time when they arrive home together after work and school. They go to their rooms, where they spend fifteen to twenty minutes alone. Serena may lie down and rest, sit in the rocking chair and listen to quiet music, or just sit in total silence with her eyes closed. Sometimes she does spiritual reading, like the Bible. Then, after that short period of time, Serena and Allyson come back together, eager to be with each other and to laugh, talk about the day's events and problems, and prepare dinner and the evening activities.

Father Joel makes a daily appointment with "Mr. B," the "B" being a bench in the nearby park. His walk over and back to Mr. B is part of his exercise regimen, and his quiet time on the bench prepares him for the rest of the afternoon and evening duties.

Some people are able to attend Mass on their way to work or at a nearby church during lunch. Others stop in a church at those times just to sit quietly and pray or meditate in their own way. More and more people begin and end each day by reading the Scriptures of the day from the lectionary. (Religious publishers or bookstores provide inexpensive resources for this purpose.) Praying with the Scriptures that the Church has chosen for us this day connects us in prayer with the Church all over the world. I often picture people in far away places using these same readings with me.

Some people use their commute time for daily prayer and reflection, by doing spiritual reading, journaling, sitting with their eyes closed (if they're not the driver!), or using the very people and life-scenes they pass as the source of their prayer. Some people who drive say they often turn off the radio to listen to what's inside of themselves. Others find it helpful to play meditative tapes of some kind.

Keeping a journal can provide another regular source of prayer and learning from life experiences. It will help you in your prayers of praise and thanksgiving as well as asking for things for which you want, like strength, guidance, insight, and wisdom. What happened today? What is the lesson here for me? Thanks to God for these blessings.

We each need to find ways to get the alone time we need. For most of us, this means revising our schedules on a regular basis, as life changes, children grow, and duties fluctuate.

• What is your routine time for daily reflection and prayer?

• Which of the examples here would you like to consider trying?

Assessment and Life Planning

Most people dread their annual evaluations with their work supervisors more than they dread their regular dental checkups. Supervisors present them with lists of shortcomings, and then salary raises are given—or not— in relation to the lists. Some of these experiences have been disguised as two-way "assessments" with two-way conversations and goal-setting times. I have come across people who shake their heads and say, "A rose by any other name."

However, there are people who actually look forward to these evaluations because the process offers supportive opportunities for growth. Rather than an exchange with a supervisor who has done the evaluation independent of the individual, these people have the opportunity to write out their own self-assessment and take stock of how they themselves think they're doing. They are then able to discuss their self-evaluation with their supervisor, compare it with the supervisor's assessment, and receive praise for work well-done and help for areas that need improvement. This model of assessment allows people a voice in setting goals for growth and development. What a difference!

Most people who have attended my workshop on staff development have heard me quote one of my favorite sages: Ed Koch, former mayor of New York. When he was my mayor he would ride the subway regularly and walk up to people along the way, shake their hand, and say, "Hi! I'm the mayor. How am I doing?"

How am I doing? While I wouldn't ask that question of strangers on the street, I would like to have it answered by someone in a position to have an informed opinion about me. In fact, I would consider that a real gift.

Life is too precious and too short to waste in doing important things poorly—but we all need help to see exactly what we're doing. We all have blind spots in our life, those areas in which we're not doing or being the person God has made us to be. We also have those wonderful moments of, in fact, being all that we can but we're oblivious to them. In the latter case, we can't acknowledge our successes, learn from them, even celebrate them, because we're not aware of them. We need the input from others to draw our attention to these moments. There is wonderful energy in that kind of encouragement, that kind of affirmation.

Aristotle is quoted as saying, "An unexamined life is a waste of time." Self-reflection, not in a self-obsessed way but with a healthy humility and honesty, can be the avenue to staying the course we have set out for ourselves. Karl Rahner said it a bit differently: "We had the experience but we missed the meaning."

Reflect alone and with another, and then take the time to acknowledge your weaknesses and celebrate your strengths. As needed, get new insights for altering your unique path of life in a small way—or occasionally in a major way so that you can come back from the detour to the main highway you want to be on.

- What are you doing really well? What do you feel good about in your life in the past year?

- Who or what has helped you with this?

- How might you honor or acknowledge or even celebrate this goodness about yourself?

- What do you want to change or improve within yourself over the coming months?

- What three things can you do to get started?

Ongoing Self-Renewal

We are social beings by nature, which means that being with others is essential to our well-being. Life, however, can sometimes interfere with our social interactions, unless we consciously bring about the things we want and need. Staying connected sustains and stimulates us. Broadening our horizons has the same effect. It can bring fresh experiences to energize us, new friends and ideas to enrich us.

Consider the following suggestions to see what interests you, and then—for your own health and wellness—renew yourself.

- Stay in touch with friends. Drop a note, send an e-mail, pick up the phone, to keep networked with people who are important to you.

- Associate with people of different ages and different backgrounds.

Some years ago, after my own daughter was grown, I started having lunch with two young brothers, family friends. These delightful adventures brought something new and fresh to my life. Added to my monthly breakfast with a group of ninety year olds, I am graced with experiences of both spontaneity and wisdom. I'm enriched by and learn from both.

• Develop a hobby that truly interests you. If you're not sure what that might be, spend time perusing the library or reading the community calendars in the newspaper or at neighborhood gathering places. Get in touch with something that you liked to do when you were younger; perhaps that interest is still there. Join a singing group, a stamp club, a hiking group; take dancing lessons, get out the old tennis racquet, join a book club.

• Participate actively in your faith community. People who belong to a faith community and have regular contact with others in small groups or in parish liturgies, organizations, and committees find these a source of sustenance and support. Connecting regularly with people who share the same values and beliefs "feeds" the soul in many ways. Always bear in mind, of course, that taking on responsibility in these groups needs to be in balance with other commitments.

• Learn something new each year. Teach yourself a foreign language by listening to an instruction tape, or check out a video each month about a different place in the world. Over the course of a year, read all the poems of your favorite poet. At one time I would subscribe to an entirely different magazine each year. One year it was *Popular Mechanics*, the next *Atlantic Monthly*, then *House Beautiful*, followed by *Sports Illustrated*.

• Be with nature. Balance in life happens only when we deliberately plan it. One of the sources for refreshment and keeping life balanced is to be in ongoing dialogue with nature. How each person does that will vary, of course. Some grow flowers, some take their lunch to a park regularly, others live where they can go to a lake or the ocean, a mountain or the woods, for refreshment. Take your family and friends on a picnic each week during the summer. Sit on the porch in the quiet of the early morning or late night. One woman who sleeps intermittently at night uses those awake times to sit at the window, open in agreeable weather, and study the sky and the motion of tree branches. A man drives to the country and walks in the farm fields there. Being with nature gives us energy, brings calm and refreshment, and helps us feel connected to the created world of which we are a part. Being with nature can connect us with the Creator like nothing else can.

- Find a mentor or be a mentor. Walking a path with another person gives us a completely different experience than walking it alone. When we are younger, we have those incredible gifts of energy, ideas, enthusiasm, and optimism. Good stewardship of those gifts uses them not just for ourselves but for others, especially for the common good. Mentors, people with more experience, or wisdom figures help the young with that process. What a waste not to make use of life experience around us. Look for someone you admire, someone who shares your values, who has made a life that you want to emulate, and spend time with that person. Most people, if asked, will be both flattered and delighted to do so. Set up a regular time such as an early morning coffee every two weeks or a lunch on Saturday or your day off. Use that time to listen, to share, to ask questions.

  If you are at the other end of life's continuum, seek out a young person you admire. Mentors are often motivated by wanting to give back, to add to the future generation though experience. However, most mentors speak of how very much they receive in return, how enriching it is to be with a person of promise. While each person is receiving something different, both are being given a gift.

- Change an old habit. Habits are formed deliberately, one step at a time, one day at a time. A new habit comes about by repeating the same action over and over until it is part of our routine, even part of ourselves. The process, though not easy, is the same, whether it's flossing our teeth, watering the flowers, playing the piano, or walking through our child's bedtime routine.

  I had a friend who worked at the hospital and needed to be there early each morning. But he was a night person by nature and would have been the last one out the door had he not deliberately, but over a period of time, developed the habit of being in bed by 10:00 P.M. He said that developing this habit wasn't easy. For months he would go to bed at 10:00 and not be able to sleep. But he created a nightly routine for himself, followed it carefully, and eventually developed a restful habit. Being asleep at 10:00 has become just a part of life for him. With a firm commitment to do something different, my friend was able to change an old habit to meet his current need. No matter where he was—at a social event, school function, or anywhere else, he would leave in time to be home. I smile when I recall meetings of a parish committee where he would stand up and announce, "It's 9:30. We said we'd meet until 9:30 so I'm leaving. I hope next month we can complete our agenda in the time we said." And he was out the door. People were startled, to say the least. The committee had developed the habit of starting late and sauntering through the agenda. Over time, they broke that habit, too, and did their work in a timely way.

Some people accomplish their goals or reform habits easily. Some need the kind of support they can find from a group process. I belonged to a professional women's club that offered a service of connecting people who wanted to be part of a "Success Team." Although the name sounded a bit pretentious, I found the process very helpful. A group of women would meet just six times—once a week or every two weeks—to act as a support-and-accountability group to help each other accomplish personal goals, change habits, or adopt new ones. For example, one person came with the goal of cleaning out the basement. Another wanted to look for a new job, and another wanted to get in the habit of walking each evening.

The process was simple. During the meeting, each woman had ten to fifteen minutes focused just on her particular goal. During that time, the woman did three things:

• She reported on how she did since the last gathering.

• She asked the group for the advice and encouragement she needed.

• She stated what she would try to accomplish before the next meeting.

These meetings provided just enough structure and social pressure to keep most of the women on track. Some need the kind of support they can find from the group process or become motivated because they've stated publicly what they're working on.

Conclusion

Being fully Christian is related to being fully human—and this is dependent upon integrating all parts of our life. "Whole" or integrated persons don't leave the gospel message in the pew when they leave church but, rather, carry it out the door and into life's decisions and interactions. Being fully human and fully Christian means integrating both our responsibilities and the various dimensions of our life: caring for ourselves while caring for others; developing and challenging ourselves while caring for our physical health and attending to our spiritual and psychological needs. God wants you "to be all that you can be." How that happens is up to you.

In their work titled *Becoming Adult/Becoming Christian,* Evelyn and James Whitehead tell us that "integrity seems to come with the considered feeling that one played the roles and met the challenges of each of the eras of the life cycle. It doesn't mean perfection; it does not mean the absence of regrets. It *does* mean having found a way to make one's life count in caring for—and hopefully enhancing—the ongoing flow of life. From the experiences one gathers, from the suffering and the gladness, one accrues the virtue Erikson calls *wisdom.*"

Those who are wise attend to their own integration throughout life, even after it becomes a habit. Those who are wise also know they don't have to do it alone.

Resources for Additional Reading

Bolman, Lee, and Terrence Deal. *Leading With Soul.* San Francisco: Jossey-Bass, 1995.

Hudson, Frederic M. and Pamela D. McLean. *Life Launch: A Passionate Guide to the Rest of Your Life.* The Hudson Institute Press, 1995.

Jamison, Kaleel. *The Nibble Theory and the Kernel of Power: A Book About Leadership, Self-Empowerment, and Personal Growth.* Mahwah, N.J., Paulist Press, 1984.